Steven Wheeler

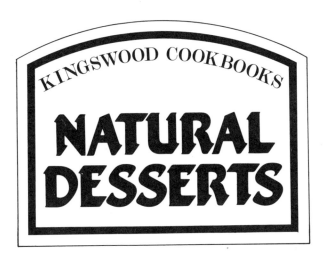

KINGSWOOD COOKBOOKS

NATURAL DESSERTS

SERIES EDITOR JUDY RIDGWAY

Photography by
NICOLA GIBBS

The Kingswood Press

CONTENTS

LIST OF ILLUSTRATIONS

INTRODUCTION

During the past few years there has arisen a new trend towards healthy living: as well as taking exercise we are now concerned about nutrition. Articles in newspapers and magazines constantly tell us of a major change in our diet. More and more people are choosing high fibre cereals and whole wheat flours, and nuts are becoming more popular than ever before. We are discovering natural sources of sugar in honey and fruit. Fruit juices, low fat yogurt, soft cheeses and fresh dairy produce are all ending up in our shopping baskets.

Our cupboards and fridges are full of these new ingredients. So what do we do with them? There are many excellent cookery books on the market covering a whole range of savoury dishes for the healthy gourmet. But what about puddings? Ideas seem to be limited and not terribly exciting.

In this book I have devised a new range of wholesome desserts to complement even the finest lunch and dinner parties. I have chosen several classic desserts from leading hotels and restaurants, many of which draw on the natural goodness of fresh fruit. Other recipes I have adjusted in view of cutting down sugar, fat and cholesterol levels, and increasing dietary fibre.

NATURAL INGREDIENTS

Flour

The most popular and by far the most versatile of cereals and grains available to us is wheat. The grain of wheat is available in almost any form, from cracked or kibbled wheat—simply cracked between rollers—to whole meal, and wheat meal flours, often stone ground in the old-fashioned way. Such flours include the full flavour and goodness of whole wheat and retain a good level of vitamins, minerals, natural oils and fibre.

During the high-speed milling of refined flour many nutrients are lost due to high temperature. In Britain highly refined flours are required by law to contain added nutrients. Although white flours are becoming less popular in home baking, they still remain useful when blending with other flours to make fine biscuits, pastries and sponges.

Bran fibre and wheat germ are the by-products of white flour. These cellulose fibres are stripped away during processing and are sold as separate products.

Fibre is the modern word for roughage. We need a certain amount of it in our diets to clean waste products from our systems. Bran is particularly rich in B vitamins, minerals and natural oils. Whole wheat and brown flours contain a good proportion of bran fibre and are essential to the high fibre diet.

Fresh fruit, dried fruit and nuts are also good sources of dietary fibre.

When fibre passes through our bodies it takes with it up to 10 per cent of the calories that we consume. So in fact by including natural fibre in our diets, we are reducing our calorie intake.

Sugar

As a race we are a mixed bunch, some of us can eat mountains of whatever we fancy, while others need only to look at food and put on weight. As we are all different it is important for us to know our limits. How many calories do we actually need, and how can we control our intake. Well, for a start, we can eliminate white sugar and products made from white sugar. As an alternative we can enjoy fresh fruits, natural brown sugars and honeys. Natural forms of sugar are more readily absorbed into our system, and produce a longer lasting release of energy. Brown sugars contain minerals—iron, calcium, phosphorus and potassium—to maintain good health. When brown sugar is purified into white sugar, all of these minerals are destroyed. Weight for weight, brown sugar contains the same amount of calories as white but because brown sugar is stronger than white we need less of it to obtain the same sweetness. Brown sugars are available in many forms; darker sugars contain raw molasses and are strong in taste. Golden granulated sugar is a good everyday brown sugar that can be substituted for white.

It is very important to differentiate between naturally brown sugars and the many refined sugars which have added caramel or molasses to give the colour. If a country of origin is given on the label, it is safe to assume it is natural sugar. If there is a list of ingredients on the pack, you can assume it is not. There are four natural brown sugars: Demarara, Light Muscovado, Muscovado or Barbados, and Molasses or Black Barbados.

The breakdown of sugars is as follows:

Molasses syrup   110 Calories per $\frac{1}{2}$ oz/128 g. Strong in flavour. Use to darken fruit cakes.
Treacle syrup   110 Calories per $\frac{1}{2}$ oz/128 g. A little less strong. Gives rich moistness to fruit cakes.
Muscavado sugar   110 Calories per $\frac{1}{2}$ oz/128 g. Strong syrupy flavour. Use in fruit cakes and puddings.
Barbados sugar   110 Calories per $\frac{1}{2}$ oz/128 g. Less strong. Use for mincemeat and fruit cakes.
Demarara sugar   110 Calories per $\frac{1}{2}$ oz/128 g. Milder flavour. Use to glaze crème brulée.
Dark brown sugar   110 Calories per $\frac{1}{2}$ oz/128 g. A softer texture, stronger in flavour. Use in fruit cakes.
Soft brown sugar   110 Calories per $\frac{1}{2}$ oz/128 g. Use when creaming with butter for sponges and cakes.
Golden sugar   110 Calories per $\frac{1}{2}$ oz/128 g. Use for syrups, old-fashioned flap jacks and slab cakes.
Golden granulated sugar   110 Calories per $\frac{1}{2}$ oz/128 g. A versatile free flowing sugar, good for general use
Granulated sugar   110 Calories per $\frac{1}{2}$ oz/128 g. As golden granulated but nutrients removed.
Caster sugar   110 Calories per $\frac{1}{2}$ oz/128 g. A quick dissolving version of white granulated.
Icing sugar   110 Calories per $\frac{1}{2}$ oz/128 g. Use for making fine biscuits and petits fours.
Honey   81 Calories per $\frac{1}{2}$ oz/128 g. Use for butter creams, syrups and sweetening fillings.
Maple syrup   100 Calories per $\frac{1}{2}$ oz/128 g. Use as for honey where its unique flavour is required.
Extract of malt   85 Calories per $\frac{1}{2}$ oz/128 g. Malt loaf and tea breads.

Honey

Honey contains 30 per cent fewer calories than cane sugar. Darker varieties are a better source of iron, copper and manganese than lighter ones. Because of the natural balance of vitamins, minerals and enzymes, honey is more readily absorbed into our bloodstream as blood sugar. Natural sugars are released more slowly into our systems as a form of sustained energy.

Spun Sugar

Spun sugar is used to decorate a variety of evening desserts.

1. Clean a heavy bottomed stainless steel or copper saucepan with hot water.
2. Moisten 1 lb 4 oz/600 g granulated sugar with 8 fl oz/240 ml water and slowly bring to boil. Make sure there are no traces of sugar on the side of the pan. If there are, brush them down using a wet pastry brush.
3. Boil syrup rapidly until temperature reaches 280°F/138°C.

4. Immerse base of the pan in cold water and allow to cool slightly. Add a little colouring.
5. Lay a measuring stick across the table so that the end is over the edge. Put some newspaper on the floor.
6. Dip the end of a twig whisk into the sugar and spin over the stick. Repeat several times.
7. Shape spun sugar into nests ready for use. Spun sugar will absorb any moisture in the air and will go soft very quickly.

Eggs and dairy produce: a natural source of protein

Fresh dairy produce has been a natural source of protein for centuries. The fine qualities of milk, cheese, butter, cream and eggs play a vital part in the balanced diet of our times. As well as being valuable sources of vitamins and minerals, the taste and texture of dairy foods are second to none.

For these reasons I have expressed a preference towards butter and other first class dairy products.

If cream has meant the end of a beautiful relationship between you and the cake shop, read on. In this book I have devised yogurt based creams, low in sugar and cholesterol.

Eggs are graded according to their size and quality. There are seven grades of egg, the smaller the number the larger the egg. Most recipes recommend grade 3 eggs as they are a uniform 60–65 g in weight. There are three classifications, A B & C. A describes fresh and naturally clean eggs. B eggs are less fresh as they have often been refrigerated for several weeks. Class C eggs are used only by food manufacturers. Free range eggs are of Class A standard and guarantee production from non battery-farmed hens and have a better flavour and contain a stronger white and a richer yolk.

Eggs should be kept cool, preferably in a larder away from strong smelling foods. If you use eggs regularly and use them in rotation they will keep for up to 10 days. If you are not intending to use them within this time they can be kept for up to 8 weeks in the refrigerator. Eggs should be kept pointed end downwards to accommodate the air pocket inside the shell. As eggs get older and less fresh this air pocket increases and will cause the egg to float in water; a good way to test the freshness of eggs. Eggs should always be used from room temperature.

Separated egg whites are always useful. They will keep for up to 1 month in a jar in the refrigerator or can be frozen for up to 6 months. One egg white constitues 30 ml. Egg yolks may be frozen for up to 3 months. Mix with a pinch of salt and seal in a container. One egg yolk can be measured as 20 ml.

Yogurt

To make yogurt:
All equipment must be sterilized.

2 pt/1.1 litre milk + 3 tablespoons milk powder
1 teaspoon live yogurt or yogurt culture

1. Bring the milk and powder to the boil. Immerse the pan in cold water, and cool the milk until hand hot (100°F/38°C).
2. Put the live yogurt into a clean bowl and stir in the warm milk.
3. Cover with a damp cloth, and leave in a warm place for 8–10 hrs. Overnight is ideal.
4. When yogurt has set, pour off any water that might have appeared on the surface.
Fresh yogurt will keep in the refrigerator for up to 10 days. Reserve a little of your own yogurt to start your next batch.

Yogurt Cheese

Yogurt cheese is used to make various low fat fillings for flans, gâteaux and pastries. The cheese will blend well with soft fruits and natural flavourings.

1. Place 40 ml low fat live yogurt in a paper coffee filter or muslin.
2. Leave to drain over a dish to 1–2 hrs.
The dish will collect the whey liquid which is then discarded.
The yogurt cheese will develop a smooth texture but a little whipped cream may be added to the cheese to add extra smoothness. Yogurt Cheese will keep up to a week in the refrigerator. It will not freeze.

Fresh and Preserved Fruits

I have chosen fresh fruit as the theme of this book, as they are an excellent source of vitamins, minerals and dietary fibre.

A fashionable way to present fruits at the table is to poach them in a light syrup and to serve them cold with yogurt or ice cream:

1 lb 8oz/700 g fruit
1 pt/600 ml water
3 oz/75 g golden granulated or soft brown sugar
½ × 50 mg tablet vitamin C (ascorbic acid)

1. Dissolve sugar and vitamin C in the water and boil for 3–4 mins.
2. Remove any scum that may appear on the surface. Flavour, if required, with lemon or orange zest, a cinnamon stick, clove, bay leaf or vanilla.
3. Put in prepared fruit, cover and simmer. Allow to cook until fruits are just tender. Large fruits such as pears will need up to 25 mins, while smaller fruits may only take a few mins. Test the fruit with a small sharp knife. Avoid overcooking the fruit as you will lose a greater proportion of the vitamins and minerals. Poached fruit will keep in the refrigerator for up to 10 days, or can be frozen for 6 months.

Apples

2.8 g Dietary fibre, 40 Calories per 4 oz/100 g
Research has shown that pectin which is found in apples can reduce levels of cholesterol in the blood and thus minimize the risk of heart disease. Apples contain essential vitamins A and C as well as potassium, calcium and magnesium.

Apples are put into cold storage around September to ensure a regular supply throughout the winter. Dessert apples are usually finished by spring. Cooking apples last a little longer. When buying apples look for a good complexion and a firm flesh. Smaller apples tend to have an improved flavour. Apples are best kept cool in the refrigerator.

Eating apples are eaten as they are or in fruit salads. Cooking varieties are sour to taste and need additional sugar. A little white wine will improve their flavour. Cooked apple will freeze for up to 6 months.

Apricots

2 g Dietary fibre, 28 Calories per 4 oz/100 g
Apricots are an excellent source of vitamin A. Fresh apricots are available from the end of May until August, and make a guest appearance around Christmas time. Dried apricots contain 24 g dietary fibre, 182 calories/100 g.

When buying fresh apricots look for smaller fruits with a slight red blush. The flesh should be firm but soft to the touch, Apricots are best kept at room temperature, they will ripen in a few days.

Bananas

3.4 g Dietary fibre, 79 Calories per 4 oz/100 g
Bananas are an energy food. They contain vitamins A, B6, and C, as well as potassium and magnesium.

Bananas are in season all year round. Dried bananas are available in health food shops. They are very sweet and something of an acquired taste.

The sweetest fresh bananas are bright yellow with flecks of dark brown on their skins. Bananas will ripen at room temperature. Never put them in the fridge or they will go black and spoil.

Blackberries

7.3 g Dietary fibre, 29 Calories per 4 oz/100 g
Blackberries are rich in potassium and magnesium and contain vitamins A, C and E.

The season is from late July to late September. Blackberries freeze for up to 3 months.

Blackcurrants

8.7 g Dietary fibre, 28 Calories per 4 oz/100 g
Blackcurrants are rich in minerals and contain vitamin C. Choose large berries of a deep colour and a thin skin.

Blueberries

6 g Dietary fibre, 60 Calories per 4oz/100 g
Blueberries are a good source of vitamin A and are a non acidic fruit, easily digested.

Blueberries are available from July to September and freeze well.

Cherries

1.5 g Dietary fibre, 47 Calories per 4 oz/100 g
In Britain there are over 30 varieties of cherry between late June and August. Poached cherries can be frozen for up to 6 months.

Raw cherries contain vitamins A & C, and potassium and magnesium are in good supply.

Dates

8.7 g Dietary fibre, 248 Calories per 4 oz/100 g
Fresh dates are a good souce of potassium and magnesium. The dried variety are naturally very sweet, contain a lot of calories and are an excellent source of dietary fibre.

Fresh dates are available from October to February. Look for large plump varieties with a good gloss. They are best kept in the refrigerator away from strong smelling foods.

Figs (Fresh)

2.5 g Dietary fibre, 41 Calories per 4 oz/100 g
Figs contain valuable minerals: potassium, calcium and magnesium and are available fresh from June to November. Both green and purple figs are very fragile and care should be taken when choosing them. The sweetest fruits have a soft flesh and a thin edible skin. Underripe figs will ripen at room temperature in a few days. Overripe fruits that seem squashy are considered the tastiest.

Gooseberries

3.2 g Dietary fibre, 17 Calories per 4 oz/100 g
Gooseberries contain vitamins A and C, potassium and calcium. English gooseberries are available from May to August. Early green varieties tend to be small and quite sour. Further into the season they ripen and develop a red tinge. Avoid overripe and squashy fruits and look for a tight, thin, almost translucent skin.

Grapes

0.9 g Dietary fibre, 61 Calories per 4 oz/100 g
Grapes are not one of the most nutritious fruits although they do contain certain trace minerals. Belgian muscat grapes are among the most prized. The best grapes are available from July to September. When choosing grapes look for a supple stem and plump fruit, with tight skins. Grapes have an improved flavour cold so keep them in the refrigerator until needed.

Grapefruit

0.3 g Dietary fibre, 11 calories per 4 oz/100 g
Grapefruit is an excellent source of vitamin C and also contains potassium, calcium and magnesium. The sweetest grapefruits are the pink variety available October to May.

Peak harvesting is between December and February. Choose grapefruits that feel heavy and have bright yellow skins and keep them in the fridge until ready for eating.

Greengage see Mirabelle

Kiwi Fruit or Chinese Gooseberry

Kiwi fruits have a high vitamin content and contain some minerals.

The season is from May to December though they are available all year round. Look for flesh which is firm to touch and avoid overripe fruits. Kiwi fruits can be ripened at home by placing them in a sealed plastic bag with an apple or a banana.

Lemons

7 Calories per 4 oz/100 g lemon juice
Vitamin C is found in both its peel and its juice. It is also a useful antiseptic, can reduce high blood pressure, prevent rheumatism, relieve colds and sore throats, combat oily skin and strengthen fingernails.

Lemons are available all year round although they are at best between November and May. Choose brightly coloured fruits that are heavy in weight. Lemons keep for several weeks in the refrigerator.

Limes

10 Calories per 4 oz/100 g lime juice
The lime has a flavour quite different from the lemon and slightly stronger. Though limes have the same nutritive value as lemons, the juice has slightly more calories. Limes are available from March to June and also around Christmastime. The best ones are dark green in colour.

Mangoes

1.5 g Dietary fibre, 59 Calories per 4 oz/100 g
Mangoes are mainly red and green with an orange blush. Ripe mangoes contain huge amounts of vitamin A & C as well as potassium. They are available from July to December but are best between August and September. Choose fruits that yield to slight pressure of the thumb. Keep ripe mangoes in the refrigerator until needed.

Melons

There are several varieties of melon available during the late summer months. Keep ripe melons in the refrigerator away from other foods.

Cantaloupe Melons
1.0 g Dietary fibre, 24 Calories per 4 oz/100 g
Cantaloupe melons are identified by their pale green netted skin, sometimes with a raised surface. The flesh is deep orange and has the fragrance of sweet roses. Ripe cantaloupes will yield to slight pressure around the stem.

Ogen Melon
1.0 g Dietary fibre, 21 Calories per 4 oz/100 g
Ogen melons have a yellow green skin with apple green flesh. They vary in size from that of a large orange to that of a grapefruit. Ripe ogens have a slightly sunken stem indicating a soft flesh.

Galia Melon
Galia Melons are round, green fleshed, with a lightly netted skin. They are sold in skin colour ranging from green to yellow, depending on the degree of ripeness.

Honeydew Melon
0.9 g Dietary fibre, 21 Calories per 4 oz/100 g
The honeydew is creamy yellow and is shaped a bit like a rugby ball. The flesh is pale green and fairly tasteless.

Water Melons
12 Calories per 4 oz/100 g
Water melons are the largest of all melons. They have an olive green skin and have a rosy pink flesh or, if Nile watermelons, a yellow flesh. Both varieties contain a lot of water hence their name. Consuming watermelon is somewhere between eating and drinking. The black seeds are harmless if swallowed.

Mirabelles and Greengages

2.5 g Dietary fibre, 43 Calories per 4 oz/100 g
Mirabelles are tiny yellow plums no bigger than a grape. Greengages are slightly larger, leaf green in colour. Both fruits are available from July to October and contain vitamins A & C as well as potassium.

Oranges

2.0 g Dietary fibre, 35 Calories per 4 oz/100 g
A medium sized orange contains our daily requirement of Vitamin C, and is also rich in potassium and calcium. The quality varies throughout the year, the best oranges are imported between October and April. Choose fruits of a bright colour. Juicy oranges are heavier in weight and have thin skins. Keep at room temperature.

Peaches

1.2 g Dietary fibre, 37 Calories per 4 oz/100 g
Peaches are rich in vitamin A and are a good source of potassium and other minerals. They are in season from June to September. Choose fruit that will yield to slight pressure of the thumb. A red blush on the peach does not necessarily indicate ripeness, and they do not ripen well with keeping. Keep in the refrigerator.

Pears

1.7 g Dietary fibre, 29 Calories per 4 oz/100 g
Pears are a good source of vitamin C and minerals. The pear season begins in September and with the help of cold storage extends well into March. Dessert pears have thin skins and a succulent flesh. Cooking pears have a thicker skin and are generally harder and quite bitter.

When buying dessert pears the flesh should yield to slight pressure around the stem. Keep ripe pears in the refrigerator.

Pineapples,

1.2 g Dietary fibre, 46 Calories per 4 oz/100 g
Pineapples are an excellent source of vitamins A & C and contain potassium, calcium and magnesium.

Pineapples are available all year round although smaller and sweeter fruits are to be found early in the year. Choose ones with yellow brown skin with eyes that are prominent, and a compact crown. Pineapples will ripen slowly at room temperature.

Plums

2.1 g Dietary fibre 38 Calories per 4 oz/100 g
There are many varieties of plum available from late summer through to about March. Victorias are the most common, they range in colour from green or yellow to near purple black. Damsons have a sharp, almost savoury, taste most suitable for jam-making.

When buying plums look for tight skins of a good colour. Plums will ripen at room temperature.

Raspberries

7.4 g Dietary fibre, 25 Calories per 4 oz/100 g
Fresh raspberries contain large amounts of potassium, calcium and magnesium, as well as vitamin C and iron.

Raspberries are in season from late June to mid August. Choose fruit that is dry as wet fruit will deteriorate rapidly. Colours vary from red to deep purple and some varieties are yellow or white. All vary in taste.

Red & White Currants

7 g Dietary fibre, 21 Calories per 4 oz/100 g
Redcurrants are valued for their high level of pectin. They yield a strong supply of vitamins A & C as well as potassium, calcium and magnesium.

All varieties of currant are in season between July and August. Look for plump fruit, bright in colour, with thin skins. Currants keep for up to a week in the refrigerator. They also freeze well.

Rhubarb

2.2 g Dietary fibre, 45 Calories per 4 oz/100 g
Rhubarb contains vitamins A & C as well as potassium and calcium. The rhubarb season begins in early February when forced varieties are available. The first outdoor rhubarb is usually ready around April. Choose young pink stems with a thin skin. Keep in the refrigerator until needed.

Strawberries

2.2 g Dietary fibre, 26 Calories per 4 oz/100 g
Bright red strawberries ripened in the sun contain large quantities of vitamin C.

The main crop of strawberries is from May to July, a second crop can be expected in October. Look for fruit that is bright in colour, preferably with 'English' written on the side of the box. Avoid wet fruits as they will deteriorate rapidly. Keep strawberries with their stalks intact until ready for eating.

Tangerines, Satsumas and Mandarins

1.9 g Dietary fibre, 34 Calories per 4 oz/100 g
Between November and February a wide selection of citrus fruits appear on the market. All such fruits are easy to peel and have a good flavour suited to the end of a meal.

Choose brightly coloured varieties that feel heavy to touch, as they are likely to contain more juice. Keep in a cool place.

Preserved Fruits

Fruits are preserved to improve their keeping qualities. Methods of preserving include drying, bottling, candying, jam making and steeping in alcohol.

Nuts

Brazil Nuts

2.5 g Dietary fibre 175 Calories per 1 oz/28 g
Brazil nuts have a mild flavour somewhere between a hazelnut and a coconut. They are very difficult to crack without breaking them, so it is best to buy them ready shelled. Brazil nuts are a good source of calcium and are rich in B vitamins. Store them in an airtight box, in a cool place.

Hazelnuts or Cobnuts

1.7 g Dietary fibre, 106 Calories per 1 oz/28 g
Hazelnuts are usually sold fresh in late autumn, when they are soft and juicy. It is better to buy hazelnuts ready shelled so you can see clearly their size and quality.

Pine Nuts

180 Calories per 1 oz/28 g
Pine nuts are the seeds from a variety of pine tree. They are creamy in colour and have a smooth soft taste.

Pistachio Nuts

3.0 g Dietary fibre, 180 Calories per 1 oz/28 g
Pistachio nuts have a very delicate flavour of almonds. Because of their strong green colour they are used mainly for decorative purposes.

Pumpkin Seeds

173 Calories per 1 oz/28 g
Pumpkin seeds are available from most health food stores. Some varieties are of an attractive olive green colour, and can be used for decoration instead of pistachio nuts. They are a good source of protein and iron.

Walnuts

1.5 g Dietary fibre, 147 Calories per 1 oz/28 g
Fresh walnuts have a tender young flesh that is yellowish green in colour. Dried walnuts can be soaked in hot milk overnight, so that a vapour is formed inside the shell which softens the flesh.

Chocolate

First class ingredients are rarely cheap, but good chocolate is worth every penny. Some good quality chocolates are: Cadbury's Bournville Dark, Chocolate Menier Pâtissier, Suchard Bittra, Callebaut, Marks & Spencer Swiss Plain

First class chocolate, known as couverture, is rich in cocoa solids, cocoa butters and natural oils retained in the cocoa bean in manufacturing. Real chocolate has a fine taste, and smell, leaving the mouth clean and fresh. Cheaper chocolates contain mainly vegetable fats. These chocolates are known as chocolate flavourings or covering chocolate.

Best eating chocolate has 150 calories per ounce and contains high percentages of fat and sugar. Cocoa powder has only 88 calories per ounce, and is free from added sugars. With this in mind it is possible to make chocolate sponges and cakes with a reduced number of calories.

Natural flavourings

Almond Essence

Make sure you buy almond essence and not almond flavouring as there is a big difference in taste.

Aniseed

Aniseed is a tiny ribbed seed ground into a powder used in making honey, bread and biscuits. In France it is distilled to make a range of popular beverages.

Cardamom

The best flavour is to be found in larger pale brown-green pods. Inside the pod are a series of small seeds of a smooth aromatic flavour.

Cinnamon

The finest cinnamon is dark in colour, and has a wildly exotic flavour.

The sticks are used mainly to enhance the flavour of poached fruits.

Powdered cinnamon is used to encourage the flavour of hazelnuts, apple purée and fruit cakes. It may be combined in equal quantities with caster sugar.

Cloves

Cloves have a strong spicy flavour. Be careful how you use them.

In a powdered form cloves are mixed in equal quantities with caster sugar and used to enhance the flavour of apples and oranges.

Coffee Essence

Dissolve some instant coffee into as little water as possible, and use sparingly. Keep in a sealed jar until needed.

Ginger

Ginger is the spicy root of a tropical plant. The root is sold in two forms: Root ginger, very strong in flavour, used mainly in savoury cooking, and stem ginger, peeled and usually preserved in sugar. Stem ginger has a milder more subtle flavour.

Ground ginger has a very strong peppery flavour and is used sparingly.

Nutmeg

Nutmeg is best when freshly grated to retain the natural oils that yield a mushy nut flavour.

Orange Flower Water

Orange flower water and Rose Water are the distilled infusions of the petals. The clear liquids have a subtle fragrance, and are used to flavour fruit cakes, turkish delight and petits fours. Along with rose water, it is found in delicatessens and Greek food shops.

Citrus Flavourings

Please do not buy citrus flavourings. A far superior flavour can be obtained directly from the fruit itself. The outer surface of the fruit or zest contains a fragrant oil that has a strong flavour. Choose brightly coloured fruits, as these have a stronger scent, and gently rub the skin on a grater. If a larger piece of zest is needed, use a vegetable peeler. A citrus zester will remove thin strips. A more delicate aroma can be obtained by rubbing the zest with a sugar lump, and dissolving the sugar in a little water.

Vanilla

Vanilla pods have a very smooth flavour, and a moist smell of syrup. They are best stored in caster or light brown sugar in a sealed glass jar. The resulting vanilla sugar is strong in flavour, and is used in many recipes. Vanilla pods can be used more than once.

Vanilla essence is an extract from the vanilla pod. This alternative is a lot cheaper than pods, and more convenient to use. Make sure you buy vanilla essence, and not vanilla flavouring.

JANUARY

Baked Apple Cheese Cake; Iced Pineapple Soufflé; Tangerine Dream;
Khoshaf; Gâteau Pithiviers; Banana and Rum Trifle;
Mincemeat and Almond Flan; Gâteau Paris Brest; Handley Oranges;
Sorbet au Poire Williamine.

BAKED APPLE CHEESE CAKE

1 × recipe Whole Meal Biscuit Pastry (see page 91)

7 oz/200 g low fat soft cheese or quark

3 oz/85 g light Muscovado sugar

1 tablespoon whole meal flour

1 egg (size 3)

2 tablespoons natural yogurt

1 tablespoon lemon juice

1 oz/25 g sultanas

pinch ground cloves

TOPPING:
2 oz/50 g whole meal flour

1 oz/25 g cool butter

1 oz/25 g light Muscovado sugar

1½ lb/675 g cooking apples

serves 6
Preheat oven 400°F/205°C/gas mark 6

1. Lightly grease a 9 in/23 cm pie dish, and line with biscuit pastry.
2. Beat together the cheese, sugar, flour, egg, yogurt, and lemon juice. Add the ground cloves and stir in the sultanas.
3. Peel, core and slice the apples. Spread a layer over the bottom of the pie dish and pour in the cheese mixture.
Arrange the remaining apples on top.
To prepare the topping:
4. Rub the cool butter into flour and sugar until they resemble fine breadcrumbs. This can be done in a food processer (1 min).
5. Sprinkle this mixture onto the pie and bake in centre of oven for 1 hr 10 mins. Test the cheese cake with a skewer. If it comes away cleanly the cake is cooked. Bon appetit!

ICED PINEAPPLE SOUFFLÉ
Illustrated on page 17

1 large pineapple

4 tablespoons Grand Marnier

3 oz/85 g golden granulated sugar

2 tablespoons clear honey

3 egg whites

10 fl oz/300 ml natural yogurt

10 fl oz/300 ml double cream

TO DECORATE:
3 oranges

3 plums

serves 8

1. Choose a 6½ in/17 cm soufflé dish. Cut a piece of card to fit around the side of the dish to raise the edge by 2 in/5 cm.
2. Trim off the top from the pineapple and save for decoration. Cut away the tough skin and remove the central core. Liquidize the flesh with Grand Marnier.
3. Put the clear honey and sugar into a heavy saucepan. Melt the sugar, over a low heat, and boil for 1½–2 mins.
4. Whisk the egg whites to a soft peak and gradually pour in the boiling sugar. Continue whisking until quite stiff.
5. Loosely whip the cream and stir in the yogurt.
6. Fold the puréed pineapple into the meringue and fold into the yogurt and cream.
Pour this mixture into the prepared soufflé dish and freeze for at least 4 hrs before serving.
Decorate with a crown of pineapple leaves, a border of orange and plum segments and a veil of spun sugar (see page 6).
Serve as an evening dessert with Tuille or Palmier Biscuits (see page 89).

TANGERINE DREAM

$1\frac{1}{2}$ lb/675 g tangerines
3 fl oz/75 ml concentrated orange juice
1oz/25 g sugar cubes
10 fl oz/300 ml double cream
5 fl oz/150 ml natural yogurt
1 teaspoon powdered gelatine

TO DECORATE:
1 oz/25 g plain chocolate

serves 6

1. Remove the fine zest from the tangerines by rubbing the skins lightly with a sugar cube.
2. Peel 2 tangerines, and reserve 18 segments for decoration.
3. Soften gelatine in 1 tablespoon cold water. (2–3 mins).
4. Squeeze the juice from the remaining tangerines into a saucepan, add the sugar cubes, and bring to the boil.
5. Remove from the heat, and stir in the softened gelatine.
Add the orange juice, and leave to cool.
6. Half whip the cream and fold in the yogurt.
7. When the orange juice is beginning to set, fold in the cream and yogurt.
Pour into 6 decorative glasses and leave to set for $1\frac{1}{2}$–2 hrs.
Garnish with segments of tangerine and flakes of dark chocolate.

KHOSHAF

Khoshaf is a Middle Eastern dessert that makes ue of a variety of dried fruits as a salad. The fruits are not stewed, rather left to macerate in the natural juices.

8 oz/225 g dried apricots
4 oz/115 g prunes
4 oz/115 g figs
2 oz/50 g raisins
2 oz/50 g dried apple
2 tablespoons clear honey
1 tablespoon orange flower water
1 teaspoon rose water
2 oz/50 g pine nuts or almonds

serves 6–8

1. Wash the fruit well and remove stalks from figs.
2. Put all the fruits into an earthenware basin, allowing room for the fruit to swell.
3. Add enough warm water to cover the fruit and stir in the honey. Add the flower water and leave to stand overnight.
Serve Khoshaf warm or cold with pistachio ice cream, and sprinkled with pine nuts.

GÂTEAU PITHIVIERS

Pithiviers is a small town about 70 km south of Paris where people enjoy this very fine almond gâteau.

1 × recipe Puff Pastry (see page 90)
1 × recipe Fine Almond Sponge (see page 94)
2 oz/50 g apricot preserve

GLAZE:
1 egg (size 3)

1 oz/25 g icing sugar

serves 6

1. Roll out the puff pastry into a rectangle 10 × 20 in/25 × 50 cm. Cut out two 9in/23 cm circles and let the circles rest for 40 mins.
2. Spread a thin layer of apricot preserve onto the first circle of puff pastry, leaving a 2 in/5 cm border.
3. Spread the filling over the pastry to a thickness of $\frac{3}{4}$ in/2 cm.
4. Brush the border with beaten egg and cover with the second piece of pastry. Glaze thinly with beaten egg, and make a pattern with a sharp knife.
5. Bake in centre oven for 40 mins.
6. Dust the surface with icing sugar and return to the oven to glaze, a further 6–8 mins.
Serve Gâteau Pithiviers warm or with pouring cream.

BANANA AND RUM TRIFLE

Lose yourself in a dream of bananas and rum soaking into a chocolate sponge with custard and yogurt cream.

1 × 8 in/20 cm Chocolate Whisk Sponge (see page 93)

4 large bananas

2 oz/50 g orange marmalade

9 fl oz/250 ml warm water

3 tablespoons clear honey

4 fl oz/100 ml dark rum

CUSTARD:
1 pt/600 ml milk

3 tablespoons custard powder

2 egg yolks

1 oz/25 g golden granulated sugar

2 drops vanilla essence

TO DECORATE:
5 fl oz/150 ml natural yogurt

5 fl oz/150 g double cream

1 oz/25 g flaked almonds

2 oz/50 g dark chocolate

1 banana

serves 8

1. Slice the sponge into three, and sandwich with orange marmalade. Cut into even cubes, and scatter into a large trifle bowl 9 in/23 cm in diameter. Add the sliced bananas.
2. Dissolve honey in warm water, and add rum.
3. Moisten the sponge with this syrup, and leave to stand.
To make the custard:
4. Dilute custard powder with 4 tablespoons cold milk.
5. Add egg yolks and stir in sugar.
6. Bring milk to boil with vanilla essence. Pour the milk over egg yolks and return to the saucepan to thicken.
Custard powder will prevent the eggs from curdling.
7. Pour custard over sponge and leave to cool.
8. Spread yogurt over the cool custard, sweeten to taste.
9. Loosely whip cream and pipe a border of rosettes around the edge.
Decorate with grated chocolate, flaked almonds and sliced bananas brushed with lemon juice.

MINCEMEAT AND ALMOND FLAN

An excellent way to use up leftover mincemeat.

1 × recipe Whole Meal Biscuit Pastry (see page 91)

3 oz/85 g mincemeat

½ × recipe Fine Almond Sponge (see page 94)

TO DECORATE:
2 oz/50 g clear honey

1 oz/25 g toasted almonds

serves 6–8
Preheat oven 400°F/205°C/gas mark 6

1. Grease an 8 in/20 cm flan ring, and line with biscuit pastry.
2. Spread the mincemeat over the bottom of the flan.
3. Prepare the almond sponge filling and spread it over the mincemeat. Bake in centre oven for 50 mins.
4. To finish brush the surface with clear honey and sprinkle with toasted almonds. Serve warm or cold with vanilla ice cream.

SORBET AU POIRE WILLIAMINE

1¾ lb/800 g first class canned pears in syrup

1 tablespoon clear honey

1 tablespoon lemon juice

2 tablespoons Eau de Vie Poire Williamine

serves 4–5

1. Liquidize pears with their syrup and then pass through a fine sieve.
2. Blend in honey, lemon juice and pear liqueur.
3. Freeze the purée in a metal basin, after 60 mins whisk to break up any pieces of ice. Return to freezer. Continue whisking every 20 mins until the sorbet is firm. (A further 1½ hrs). If the sorbet becomes too hard leave in the refrigerator for 20 mins prior to serving.
Serve the sorbet in stem glasses and top with a little more pear liqueur.
Offer Langues des Chats biscuits at the table (see page 88).

GÂTEAU PARIS BREST

This pastry delight commemorates the staging of a bicycle race from Paris to Brest. Every year riders compete for the major accolade.

1 × recipe choux Pastry (see page 92)
COFFEE FILLING:
10 fl oz/300 ml milk
2 egg yolks (40 ml)
1 oz/25 g light Muscovado sugar
4 tablespoons plain flour
1 tablespoon instant coffee powder
5 fl oz/150 ml double cream

serves 8
Preheat oven 400°F/205°C/gas mark 6

1. Lightly grease a 9 in/23 cm flan ring and place it on a greased baking sheet.
2. Prepare the choux pastry and fill a piping bag fitted with a large plain $\frac{1}{2}$ in/12 mm tube.
3. Pipe a broad ring inside the prepared flan ring. Remaining pastry can be used to make eclairs or bun shapes.
Cooked choux pastry freezes well (6–8 weeks).
4. Brush the choux pastry ring with beaten egg or milk.
Sprinkle on the flaked almonds and bake near the top of the oven for at least 45 mins. The most common fault with choux pastry is underbaking, so please ensure the pastry is properly cooked.
To prepare the filling:
5. Whisk together the egg yolks and sugar with 3 tablespoons of milk.
6. Add the flour and whisk until smooth.
7. Bring the remaining milk to the boil with the instant coffee.
8. Pour the boiling milk over the eggs and return to the saucepan. Stir back to the boil and allow to thicken.
9. When the filling is completely cool, loosely whip the cream and blend into the filling.
10. Split the choux pastry ring in half and pipe or spoon in the coffee cream. Replace the lid and dust with icing sugar. Serve Gâteau Paris Brest at luncheon, tea or dinner. It is best eaten on the day of making.

HANDLEY ORANGES

Handley Oranges have a smooth aromatic flavour of honey and spice. Easy to prepare and welcomed as a lunchtime dessert.
Illustrated on page 17

6 small oranges
1 pt/600 ml boiling water
3 oz/75 g light Muscovado sugar
3 tablespoons clear honey
2 cloves
4 cardamom pods
1 cinnamon stick
1 bay leaf
8 whole allspice

serves 8

1. Wash the oranges well, and score them from top to bottom with a cannelle knife. Cut the oranges into even slices, $\frac{1}{4}$ in/6 mm wide.
2. Prepare a syrup from the sugar, honey and water.
Add the spices and simmer the oranges for 20–25 mins over a gentle heat.
Serve Handley Oranges warm or cold with pouring cream or yogurt.
The orange slices will keep in the refrigerator for up to 10 days, and will improve in flavour.

FEBRUARY

Pancakes (Apple and Date, Banana with Dark Rum, Crêpes Madame);
Fresh Orange Sorbet; Chocolate and Orange Mousse;
Manchester Pie; Valentine Cake; Banana and Pineapple Flan;
Coupe Lion Heart; Passion Fruit Sorbet.

PANCAKES

The French enjoy the sheer elegance of wafer thin crêpes
enclosing a host of fruit fillings. In England, Shrove Tuesday,
the day before the beginning of Lent, is as good an excuse as
any to get out the frying pan. I have suggested a few
favourite fillings.

BASIC PANCAKE BATTER:

4 oz/115 g whole meal flour

8 fl oz/250 ml milk

2 eggs (size 3)

1 tablespoon clear honey

½ orange (zest)

½ oz/15 g butter

Makes 12 pancakes

Pancake batter is best made by hand.
However if you wish to use your food
processor, use the blade attachment.
To make the batter:
1. Sieve flour into a mixing bowl, include the
remaining bran.
2. Add ⅓ of the milk to the flour and whisk
into a smooth paste.
3. Add the rest of the milk, the eggs, honey
and orange zest.
4. Melt the butter in a frying pan, and allow
to burn slightly.
The French call this preparation beurre
noisette because of its nutty aroma.
5. Add the butter to the pancake batter. The
batter should be the consistency of single
cream.
6. Sieve, and leave to stand for at least 10
mins before using.
To make the pancakes:
7. Heat the frying pan over a steady heat.
If you have a non-stick pan, it is not
necessary to use extra oil when cooking.
8. Pour enough batter into the frying pan to
just coat the bottom.
9. Leave for a few seconds, carefully lift the
edge with a palette knife, and turn over
quickly.
10. Allow pancakes to colour slightly, before
turning onto a cloth.

Pancakes are best eaten fresh. If however
you are planning to make pancakes for a
dinner party next weekend, prepare them
today, place between sheets of greaseproof
paper and freeze. Pancakes freeze for up to 3
weeks and will thaw almost immediately.

APPLE AND DATE PANCAKES

1 × recipe Pancakes (see page 16).

FILLING:
1 oz/25 g unsalted butter

1 lb/450 g dessert apples, peeled cored and sliced

1 oz/25 g light Muscovado sugar

½ teaspoon mixed spice

3 oz/85 g fresh dates (chopped)

2 tablespoons dry white wine

1 oz/25 g flaked almonds (toasted)

15 fl oz/450 g natural yogurt to serve

serves 4–6
Preheat oven 325°F/160°C/gas mark 3

1. Melt butter in a frying pan and allow to
brown slightly.
2. Throw in apples, sugar, spice and dates,
add white wine, allow to simmer until apples
are tender, 3–4 mins.
3. Place a little of the filling on each pancake
and roll up neatly.
Arrange them in an ovenproof dish.
4. Cover with foil and keep warm in the
oven for 25–30 mins.
Sprinkle with toasted almonds, serve with
natural yogurt or vanilla ice cream.

Iced Pineapple Souffle
Recipe on page 12

Handley Oranges
Recipe on page 15

BANANA PANCAKES WITH DARK RUM

1 × recipe Pancakes (see page 16).

2 ripe bananas, thinly sliced

a little dark rum

15 fl oz/450 ml low fat yogurt

2 oz/50 g dark Muscovado or Barbados sugar

serves 4–6
Preheat oven 325°F/160°C/gas mark 3

1. Cover the bottom of the frying pan with the pancake mixture.
2. Arrange the slices of banana onto the pancake.
3. Turn over and allow to colour before turning onto a clean tea towel.
4. Sprinkle each pancake with a little dark sugar and douse with rum.
Fold into 4 and arrange in an ovenproof dish.
Cover with foil, and keep warm in the oven for 25–30 mins.
Serve 2–3 per person with natural yogurt.

CRÊPES MADAME

Fresh pineapple laced with Cointreau, bound in a velvet sauce. An experience to be shared with the closest of friends.

1 × recipe Pancakes (see page 16).

1 small pineapple

3 tablespoons Cointreau

10 fl oz/300 ml natural yogurt

1 heaped tablespoon cornflour,

1 egg (size 3)

1 oz/25 g light Muscavado sugar

2 pt/1.1 litre Fresh Orange Sorbet

serves 4–6
Preheat oven 325°F/160°C/gas mark 3

1. Cut the pineapple into small pieces and leave to macerate in the Cointreau (5–10 mins).
2. Put the yogurt in a saucepan.
3. Dilute the cornflour with a little cold water and separate the egg yolk into the cornflour.
4. Whisk the cornflour into the yogurt, bring to the boil and allow to thicken.

5. Whisk the egg white with the sugar until firm.
6. Gently fold the egg white into the boiling yogurt.
7. Add the pineapple and Cointreau.
8. Place a little of this filling onto each pancake, roll up and arrange in an ovenproof dish.
9. Cover with foil and keep warm in the oven 25–30 mins.
Serve with Orange Sorbet and a little more Cointreau.

FRESH ORANGE SORBET

9 large oranges

8 oz/225 g golden granulated sugar

serves 6
Adjust your freezer to its coldest setting.
1. Remove the zest from 3 oranges with a fine grater.
2. Squeeze the juice of 9 oranges into a measuring jug.
3. Adjust the volume to 24 fl oz/700 ml with water.
4. Measure 7 fl oz/200 ml of the liquid into a saucepan.
Add the sugar and orange zest.
Bring to the boil and simmer for 5 mins.
Add the remaining orange juice and allow to cool completely.
Strain the syrup into a metal bowl and put into the freezer for 60 mins. Whisk the sorbet every 20 mins until firm (a further 1½ hr).
If the sorbet has become hard, place it in the refrigerator for 20 mins before serving.
Offer langues des chats biscuits as an accompaniment (see page 88).
Ice cream machines are much quicker and produce a better textured sorbet.

CHOCOLATE AND ORANGE MOUSSE

7 oz/200 g plain chocolate

4 eggs, separated

2 tablespoons clear honey

10 fl oz/300 ml double cream

TO DECORATE:
5 fl oz/150 ml whipping cream

2 oz/50 g dark chocolate

1 orange (zest)

serves 8

1. Break up the chocolate, and melt it over a saucepan of hot water. Finely grate the zest of orange into the chocolate.
2. Add egg yolks to the melted chocolate, and blend together.
3. Whisk egg whites with the clear honey until they form soft peaks.
4. Carefully fold the beaten egg whites into the chocolate with a large metal spoon. Loosely whip the cream, and fold in gently to retain as much air as possible.
Pour the mousse into 8 serving glasses, and decorate with a rosette of whipped cream, and flakes of dark chocolate.
The mousse will keep in the refrigerator for up to 24 hrs before serving.

MANCHESTER PIE

The sublety of a baked egg custard unites itself with a delicate almond sponge to make this lunchtime dessert, a great family favourite.

1 × recipe Fine Almond Sponge (see page 94)

CUSTARD:
1 pt/600 ml milk

3 eggs (size 3)

1 tablespoon golden granulated sugar

TO DECORATE:
2 oz/50 g toasted flaked almonds

serves 6
Preheat oven 400°F/200°C/gas mark 6

To prepare the egg custard:
1. Break the eggs into a basin and add the sugar.
2. Bring the milk to the boil and whisk over the eggs.
3. Spread the almond sponge filling into the bottom of 2 pt/1 litre pie dish.

Sieve the egg custard over the filling.
This may seem a little strange, but when the pie is cooked, the almond sponge will be on top and the custard underneath. Don't worry it always works.
4. Bake in centre oven for 30–50 mins.
Serve Manchester Pie warm with poached fruit and a little single cream on special occasions.

VALENTINE CAKE

On 14th February we give all sorts of things to our lovers. Arrow shooting Cupids, pink elephants and clueless cards. Why not make yours an offer they cannot refuse?

1 × recipe Rich Dark Chocolate Sponge (see page 94). made in a 1 × 7 in/18 cm heart shaped cake tin.

CHOCOLATE CHEESE FILLING:
5 oz/140 g low fat soft cheese or quark

5 fl oz/150 ml single cream

1 tablespoon clear honey

3 oz/85 g plain chocolate (melted)

TOPPING:
2 egg whites

3 tablespoons golden granulated sugar

edible red colouring

5 fl oz/150 ml orange juice

3oz/85 g orange marmalade

1. Slice the sponge into 3 with a serrated knife.
Moisten each layer with orange juice and spread with orange marmalade; a little dark rum won't go amiss.
To prepare the chocolate filling:
2. Blend the cream into the soft cheese, add the clear honey, and stir in the melted chocolate. Avoid over mixing.
3. Sandwich the layers of sponge with the filling.
To prepare the topping:
4. Whisk the egg white together with the sugar to form a stiff peak. Colour the meringue a soft pink with a drop of red food colouring. Be careful not to add too much.
5. Cover the top surface.
6. Colour the remaining meringue red and make an inscription. Decorate with 2 red candles and a large red ribbon.

Banana and Pineapple Flan

BANANA AND PINEAPPLE FLAN

1 × recipe Sweet Shortcrust Pastry (see page 90).

1 small pineapple

2 ripe bananas

3 oz/75 g apricot preserve

FILLING:
2 level tablespoons cornflour

5 fl oz/150 ml cold milk

2 egg yolks

2 tablespoons light Muscovado sugar

5 fl oz/150 g natural yogurt

3 drops vanilla essence

serves 6

Preheat oven 400°F/205°C/gas mark 6

1. Lightly grease a 9 in/23 cm flan ring, and line with shortcrust pastry. Rest for 30 mins and bake blind for 25–30 mins.

To prepare the filling:
2. Dilute the cornflour with 4 tablespoons of the cold milk.
3. Stir in egg yolks, sugar and yogurt. Bring the remaining milk to the boil with vanilla essence and pour over the eggs, sugar and yogurt.
4. Return to the saucepan and stir back to the boil to thicken.
5. Spread the yogurt filling into the baked flan case and leave to cool.
6. Cut away the tough skin of the pineapple with a serrated knife.
Remove the centre core with an apple corer. Thinly slice the pineapple and cut into even pieces.
7. Arrange the pineapple with alternating layers of sliced banana towards the middle.
8. Dilute the apricot preserve with 1 tablespoon water, bring to the boil and glaze flan thinly with a flat brush.
Banana and Apricot Flan is best enjoyed the day made. Does not freeze well.

Coupe Lion Heart

PASSION FRUIT SORBET

8 oz/225 g ripe passion fruit

3 oz/85 g golden granulated sugar

5 fl oz/150 ml water

serves 4–5
Adjust your freezer to its coldest setting.

1. Cut the passion fruits in half and empty the flesh into a food processor. Liquidize the pulp to loosen the black seeds. Reserve the shells as you may wish to serve the sorbet inside them.
2. Sieve the juice into a stainless steel saucepan.
Add the sugar and water. Simmer for 5 mins and allow to cool completely before freezing.
3. Put the syrup into a metal basin and freeze for 60 mins. Then whisk the sorbet every 20 mins until quite firm (a further $1\frac{1}{2}$ hr). Serve Passion Fruit Sorbet in the shells set onto a plate with Langues des Chats biscuits as an accompaniment (see page 88). If the sorbet becomes too hard in the freezer, leave it to thaw for 20 mins in the refrigerator before serving.

COUPE LION HEART
For your Valentine.

10 fl oz/300 ml Passion Fruit Sorbet

2 oz/50 g redcurrant jelly

2 splashes apricot brandy

2 heart shaped biscuits (see Whole Meal Biscuit Pastry, page 91)

serves 2

1. Choose 2 attractive glasses, dip the rims in a little egg white and then into caster sugar.
2. Prepare sauce by thinning the redcurrant jelly with a drop of brandy.
3. Put the sorbet into the prepared glasses. Pour over the sauce and decorate with a heart shaped biscuit.
As you serve the coupe, pour over a little apricot brandy.

Dutch Apple Flan; Ananas Georgette;
Orange and Lemon Cheese Cake; Apple and Rhubarb Streusel;
Tarte Tatin; Poires Belle Époque; Petits Pots Perciville;
Banana Suédoise.

DUTCH APPLE FLAN

1 × recipe Whole Meal Biscuit Pastry (see page 91)

2 lb/900 g English dessert apples

1 tablespoon lemon juice

1 teaspoon ground cinnamon

pinch mixed spice

½ × 50 g tablet ascorbic acid (vitamin C)

2 oz/50 g sultanas

1–2 tablespoons soft brown sugar

TO GLAZE:
3 oz/85 g apricot preserve.

serves 6
Preheat oven 400°F/205°C/gas mark 6

1. Lightly grease an 8 in/20 cm flan ring and line with biscuit pastry. Half bake the flan blind for 20 mins.
2. Peel and core half the apples.
Cook to a purée with the lemon juice and vitamin C, Vitamin C, ascorbic acid, will maintain perfect whiteness during cooking. Add the sultanas and sugar to sweeten.
3. Spread the purée into the half baked flan case.
4. Wash core and slice the remaining apples. Arrange them in a flower pattern over the purée.
5. Bake the flan on the top of the oven for 25–30 mins.
To glaze:
6. Dilute the apricot preserve with 1 tablespoon water. Bring to the boil and glaze thinly with a flat brush.
Serve warm with vanilla ice cream or yogurt.

ANANAS GEORGETTE

Little pineapple mousses with an apricot sauce.

1 × recipe Fine Almond Sponge (see page 94).

juice of 3 oranges

2 oz/50 g white marzipan

1 tablespoon powdered gelatine

5 fl oz/150 ml natural yogurt

2 tablespoons Kirsch or Cointreau

5 fl oz/150 ml double cream

1 small pineapple

1 small tin (8 oz/225 g) whole apricots in natural fruit juice

serves 6

1. Cut 6 pieces of almond sponge to fit inside 6 × 3 in/8 cm ring moulds. Pieces of card board tube are a useful alternative.
2. Squeeze the juice of 3 oranges (8 fl oz/200 ml) into a stainless steel saucepan. Bring to the boil and dissolve the marzipan.
3. Soften the gelatine into 3 tablespoons cold water (2–3 mins).
4. Draw the saucepan away from the heat and stir the soft gelatine into the marzipan mixture.
Allow this preparation to cool completely.
5. Add the yogurt and stir in the Kirsch or Cointreau.
6. Loosely whip the cream and fold into the setting mousse.
7. Pour the mousse into the prepared moulds and set in the refrigerator for 1½–2 hrs.
Cut the pineapple into thin slices and trim to fit the tops of the mousses.
To prepare the sauce:
8. Reserve 6 halves of apricot for decoration. Liquidize the remaining apricots together with their own syrup and pass through a fine sieve.
To serve:
9. Turn each mousse out of its mould and arrange a piece of pineapple onto each. Decorate with half an apricot and a few pines from the pineapple. Serve each mousse on a large plate and surround with apricot sauce.

ORANGE AND LEMON CHEESE CAKE
Illustrated on page 24

3 oranges
2 lemons
7 oz/200 g low fat soft cheese or quark
5 fl oz/150 ml natural yogurt
5 oz/140 g whipping cream
0.4 oz/11 g gelatine
1 egg (size 3)
1 egg yolk
2 tablespoons clear honey

BISCUIT BASE:
4 oz/115 g digestive biscuits
2 oz/50 g butter

TOPPING:
2 tablespoons soft brown sugar
2 level teaspoons cornflour

TO DECORATE:
1 kiwi fruit
3 oranges
4 oz/115 g dark grapes

serves 8

1. Line an 8 in/20 cm loose-bottomed cake tin with greaseproof paper.
2. Crush digestive biscuits in a plastic bag or whizz them in a food processor.
3. Melt the butter in a saucepan and stir in the crumbs.
Press into the bottom of the tin and leave to cool.
To prepare the cheese:
4. Finely grate the zest from 2 oranges and 2 lemons.
Add to the soft cheese and stir in the yogurt (food processor 20 secs).
5. Loosely whip the cream and fold into the cheese mixture.
Soften the gelatine in 2 tablespoons cold (water 2–3 mins).
Melt the gelatine over a saucepan of boiling water.
6. Whisk the egg and the egg yolk together with the honey until a thick ribbon can be drawn across the surface.
7. Add the melted gelatine to the cheese mixture and fold in the beaten eggs with a large metal spoon.

8. Pour the setting cheese into the prepared cake tin, and leave to set in the refrigerator for 2–3 hrs.
To prepare the topping:
9. Segment the oranges with a sharp knife. Reserve the juice in a small basin.
Squeeze the juice of 2 lemons into a stainless steel saucepan and add the orange juice. Add the sugar and bring to the boil.
10. Dilute the cornflour with 4 teaspoons cold water, stir into the liquid and simmer to thicken.
When the cheese cake has set, spread the topping over the surface.
Allow to cool completely before releasing the mould.
Decorate the top with orange segments, kiwi fruit and black grapes. Orange and Lemon Cheese Cake will keep in the refrigerator for up to 4 days. Will freeze for up to 2 months.

APPLE AND RHUBARB STREUSEL

1 lb/450 g bramley apples
10 oz/285 g rhubarb
1 oz/25 g stem ginger
2 oz/50 g soft brown sugar

STREUSEL TOPPING:
2 oz/50 g whole meal flour
2 oz/50 g rolled oats
2 oz/50 g soft brown sugar
2 oz/50 g cool butter

serves 4–5
Preheat oven 375°F/190°C/gas mark 5

1. Peel, core and slice the apples into a 2 pt/1 litre pie dish. Peel the rhubarb and cut into even lengths.
2. Cut the stem ginger into small pieces and put into the pie dish with the brown sugar. Add 2 tablespoons cold water.
To prepare the streusel topping:
3. Rub all of the ingredients together to form a fine crumb consistency. (1 min in a food processor).
4. Sprinkle the streusel topping over the fruit, and bake in centre oven for 40–45 mins.
Serve Apple and Rhubarb Streusel warm, with vanilla ice cream or custard sauce.
Streusel is favoured as a lunchtime dessert.

Orange and Lemon Cheesecake
Recipe on page 23

TARTE TATIN

A classic taste of northern France, also known as upside-down apple pie.

4 oz/115 g Puff Pastry (see page 90)
2 lb/900 g English dessert apples
2 oz/50 g Normandy butter
2 oz/50 g golden granulated sugar
1 tablespoon lemon juice
½ teaspoon ground cinnamon

serves 6
Preheat oven 400°F/205°C/gas mark 6

1. Roll out the pastry to a 10 in/25 cm square, and rest it for ¾ hr.
2. Peel, core and quarter the apples. Fry them a few at a time in butter. Transfer onto a paper towel.
3. Put the sugar into the frying pan and moisten with 2 tablespoons water. Allow the sugar to caramelize over a gentle heat (3–4 mins).
4. Pour into an 8 in/20 cm × 2in/5 cm deep cake tin
5. Arrange the apple quarters into the tin, add the lemon juice and sprinkle on the cinnamon.
6. Cut the pastry into a 10 in/25 cm circle and place over the apples. Bake in the centre oven for 45 mins.
7. Turn the tin upside-down onto the serving dish and release the apples onto the pastry base.
Serve Tarte Tatin warm, with vanilla ice cream, pouring cream, or yogurt.
Tarte Tatin is at its most delicious as it comes out of the oven, although it will keep for up to 24 hous.
May be frozen prior to baking in the tin for up to 8 weeks.

Poires Belle Epoque

POIRES BELLE ÉPOQUE

Poire Belle Epoque presents a perfect balance of apricots, almonds and pine nuts, hidden away inside a beautifully poached pear. A perfect end to a lively dinner party.

6 small ripe pears
1½ pt/850 ml water
5 oz/140 ml golden granulated sugar
1 lemon
1 cinnamon stick
2 pt/1.1 litre Vanilla Ice Cream (see page 64)
2 oz/50 g flaked almonds
FILLING: 8 oz/225 g dried apricots
2 oz/50 g white marzipan
1 oz/25 g pine nuts

serves 6

1 Peel pears whole and remove the core, from the underside with a melon baller.
2. Prepare a syrup from the water, sugar, lemon and cinnamon.
Poach the pears in syrup for 20–30 mins depending on their ripeness. Remove pears.
3. Cook half of the apricots in the pear syrup, 15–20 mins, and purée in a food processor. Adjust the purée to a smooth sauce with ½ pt/300 ml of the pear syrup and leave to cool.
4. Chop remaining apricots and blend with the marzipan. Adjust with a little apricot sauce until smooth. Add the pine nuts and stuff the inside cavity of each pear with the filling.
Serve each pear with a ball of vanilla ice cream and a cordon of apricot sauce. Decorate with a small rosette of whipped cream and a few flaked almonds.

PETIT POTS PERCIVILLE

Little egg custards with bananas and dark rum.

4 eggs (size 3)

1 tablespoon clear honey

1 pt/600 ml milk

3 ripe bananas

1 fl oz/30 ml brandy

TO GLAZE:
2 oz/50 g apricot preserve

pistachio nuts to decorate

serves 6
Preheat oven 400°F/205°C/gas mark 6

1. Choose 6 little soufflé dishes, preferably white, and arrange them on a suitable roasting tray.
2. Break the eggs into a basin and beat them together with the clear honey.
3. Bring the milk to the boil and pour over the eggs.
4. Strain the custard into a jug and ¾ fill the soufflé dishes.
5. Fill the roasting tray with boiling water and cover over with a baking sheet. This will prevent a skin from forming on the custards while cooking.
6. Bake the custards in the middle of a preheated oven for 25–30 mins. Allow the custards to cool before decorating.
7. Slice the bananas thinly, moisten them with brandy and arrange over each custard. Dilute the apricot preserve with 1 tablespoon water. Bring to the boil and glaze the custards thinly with a flat brush.
Decorate each with half a pistachio nut.
Chill well before serving.

BANANA SUÉDOISE

1 tablet lime jelly

2 large bananas

2 limes

3 teaspoons powdered gelatine

5 fl oz/150 ml double cream

2 oz/50 g golden granulated sugar

5 fl oz/150 ml natural yogurt

2 eggs (size 3)

1½ lb/675 g seasonal fruits

4 fl oz/100 ml orange juice

serves 6

1. Make up jelly using half the recommended water. Set a thin layer into the bottom of an 8 in 20 cm ring mould.
2. Slice the bananas and arrange them on the jelly. Pour in enough jelly to cover the bananas and leave to set once more. Set the remaining jelly in a small bowl.
To prepare the mousse:
3. Remove the zest from 2 limes with a citrus zester and soften in boiling water for 2–3 mins.
4. Squeeze the juice into a small cup, add the powdered gelatine and leave to soften (2–3 mins).
Melt over a saucepan of boiling water.
5. Loosely whip cream with 1 oz/25 g sugar. Add lime zest and blend with yogurt.
6. Separate the eggs. Stir yolks into cream and whisk whites with remaining sugar to form soft peaks.
7. Whisk gelatine into cream and fold in beaten egg whites. Pour into the prepared ring mould and refrigerate for 2–3 hrs.
8. Prepare the fruit salad and moisten with a little orange juice.
9. Cut the remaining jelly into small cubes.
10. Dip the ring mould into warm water and turn out onto a serving dish.
Arrange the fruit salad in the centre, and the jelly cubes around the outside.

APRIL

Rhubarb and Custard Flan; Old English Syllabub;
Soufflé Glacé au Grand Marnier; Carrot and Hazelnut Gâteau;
Conversation Gâteau; Honey and Lime Bananas;
Crème Negretta; Soft Caramel Pears; Devonshire Junkets;
Tutti Frutti Yogurt Ice; Rhubarb and Ginger Yogurt Ice;
Pecan and Molasses Scones.

RHUBARB AND CUSTARD FLAN

12 oz/350 g Whole Meal Biscuit Pastry (see page 91)

1 lb/450 g young rhubarb

5 fl oz/150 ml single cream

1 teaspoon clear honey

2 eggs (size 3)

TO GLAZE:
3 oz/75 g apricot preserve

serves 6
Preheat oven 375°F/190°C/gas mark 5

1. Lightly grease an 8 in/20 cm flan ring, and line with biscuit pastry.
2. Peel rhubarb, and cut into 1½ in/4 cm lengths.
Arrange the rhubarb into the flan in rows that overlap each other.
3. Prebake the flan with the rhubarb near the bottom of the oven for 35 mins.
To prepare the custard:
4. Stir honey into single cream, and beat in eggs. Strain the custard through a fine sieve, and pour over the pre-baked flan.
5. Return the flan to the top shelf of the oven for a further 10–15 mins until the custard has set lightly on the top.
Allow the flan to cool on a wire rack.
To glaze:
6. Dilute apricot preserve with 1 tablespoon water, bring to the boil and glaze thinly with a flat brush.
Serve Rhubarb and Custard Flan warm or cold as a lunchtime dessert.
Rhubarb Flan will keep for up to 24 hrs in the refrigerator, it does not freeze well.

OLD ENGLISH SYLLABUB

A delightful tradition with an old English taste of good brandy.

1 orange

1 lemon

2 fl oz/50 ml brandy

10 fl oz/300 ml double cream

1 tablespoon clear honey

7 oz/200 g low fat soft cheese or quark

TO DECORATE:
2 oranges

2 lemons

1 tablespoon icing sugar

serves 8

1. Finely grate the zest from the orange and lemon into a basin.
Squeeze in juice, add brandy and leave for at least 2 hours to marinate.
2. Loosely whip the cream with honey.
Blend in the soft cheese, stir in the brandy and citrus juices.
3. Divide the syllabub between 8 stem glasses and chill well.
To prepare the decoration:
4. Remove the zest from the oranges and lemons with a citrus zester.
Blanch the thin strands in boiling water for 8–10 mins.
Spread the zest pieces onto a baking sheet and sprinkle with icing sugar.
Put the baking sheet under a hot grill for 3–4 mins until the sugar has caramelized and the zest has become like straw.
This garnish will keep for several months in an airtight jar.
Old English Syllabub will keep for up to 8 hrs in the refrigerator. After this time the brandy may begin to separate. Offer Savoy Biscuits as an accompaniment (see page 89).

Carrot and Hazelnut Gateau

CARROT AND HAZELNUT GÂTEAU

Beautifully moist, made without any flour or fat.

CARROT SPONGE:
7 oz/200 g finely grated carrot

7 oz/200 g ground hazelnuts

1 teaspoon ground cinnamon

5 oz/140 g golden granulated sugar

4 eggs (size 3)

FILLING:
4 oz/115 g soft unsalted butter

1 tablespoon clear honey

TO DECORATE:
6 oz/170 g white marzipan

8 whole hazelnuts

1 oz/25 g angelica

1 oz/25 g cocoa powder

serves 8
Preheat oven 400°F/205°C/gas mark 6

1. Finely grate carrots and mix with ground hazelnuts and cinnamon.
2. Warm the sugar on a small ovenproof plate 6–8 mins, in the oven.
3. Meanwhile lightly grease a 9 in/23 cm sponge tin, cut a circle of greaseproof paper to fit the bottom of the tin and dust the whole tin with flour.
4. Break eggs into a clean bowl and add the warmed sugar. Whisk the eggs until a thick ribbon can be drawn across the surface (10–12 mins).
5. Carefully fold in the carrots and hazelnuts with a large metal spoon. Avoid overmixing or you will destroy the lightness. Turn into the prepared tin and bake in centre of oven for 35–40 mins.
6. Turn the sponge upside-down onto a cooling wire.
To prepare the filling:
7. Beat butter with honey until pale and quite fluffy. This is best done with an electric mixer.
8. Cut the carrot sponge in half and sandwich with some filling. Cover the sides and top with a very thin layer of filling.
9. Colour $\frac{3}{4}$ marzipan brown and the remaining $\frac{1}{4}$ carrot orange. Cover the top of the gâteau with a thin layer of brown marzipan and fashion 8 small carrots from

the orange colour. Roll the 'carrots' in a little cocoa powder to improve their appearance. Cut a small piece of angelica to fit the end of each carrot and arrange the carrots around the gâteau with the hazelnuts.
Chill and serve for Easter lunch or tea.

CONVERSATION GÂTEAU

$\frac{1}{2}$ × recipe Puff Pastry (see page 90)

1 × recipe Fine Almond Sponge (see page 94)

TO GLAZE:
1 egg (size 3)

$\frac{1}{2}$ teaspoon salt

TO FINISH:
2 oz/50 g icing sugar

serves 6–8
Preheat oven 400°F/205°C/gas mark 6

1. Roll out puff pastry into a rectangle 10 × 12 in/25 × 50 cm.
Cut out two circles 9 in/23 cm in diameter, and rest them in the refrigerator with the trimmings for at least 40 mins.
2. Soften icing sugar with $\frac{1}{2}$ teaspoon cold water to form a smooth icing, spread a thin layer of icing onto one of the circles of puff pastry. Cut the trimmings into thin strips and lay them over the icing in a criss cross design.
3. Spread a thin layer of apricot preserve over the second circle of pastry to within $1\frac{1}{2}$ in/4 cm of the edge.
Spread a good layer of almond sponge filling over the preserve.
4. Brush the edge thinly with beaten egg and sandwich with the second circle.
5. Bake in centre oven for 40–45 mins.
Enjoy Conversation Gâteau while it is still warm with vanilla ice cream. Or serve cold with tea or coffee.
The perfect conversation piece.
Freezes well before baking, 2–3 months.

HONEY AND LIME BANANAS

A quick and easy dessert, very popular with young children

4 limes

3 tablespoons honey

4 crushed cardamom pods

6 large bananas

TO SERVE:
2 pt/1.1 litre vanilla ice cream
    or 18 fl oz/450 ml natural yogurt

serves 6

1. Remove the zest from the limes with a citrus zester.
2. Measure 1 pt/300 ml water into a stainless steel saucepan. Add the lime zest, squeeze in the juice and stir in the honey. Bring the syrup to the boil. Add the crushed cardamom pods and simmer for 5 mins.
3. Cut the bananas into even pieces, or leave them whole.
Arrange in a basin, and pour the boiling syrup over the fruit.
4. Leave the bananas to cook slowly in their own heat until cool.
Honey and Lime Bananas will keep for up to 1 week in the refrigerator. They do not freeze well.
Serve with vanilla ice cream or natural yogurt.

CRÈME NEGRETTA

10 fl oz/300 ml milk

5 fl oz/150 ml double cream

4 oz/115 g good dark chocolate

2 egg yolks

1 egg (size 3)

2 tablespoons clear honey

3 tablespoons dark rum

TO DECORATE:
5 fl oz/150 ml whipped cream

6 chocolate curls

serves 6
Preheat oven 375°F/190°C/gas mark 5

1. Bring the milk to boil with the cream, withdraw from heat, and stir in the chocolate.
2. Separate the egg yolks into a basin, add the whole egg, honey and rum.
3. Pour the hot milk over the eggs, and pass through a fine sieve.
4. Arrange 6 small soufflé dishes in a high-sided roasting tray. Fill the dishes ⅔ full with the mixture, and ½ fill the roasting tray with boiling water.
Cover the whole tray with a baking sheet and bake in the bottom of oven for 20–25 mins.
When the point of a small knife comes away cleanly the custards are cooked.
5. Chill the custards well, and decorate with a rosette of whipped cream and a chocolate curl.
Crème Negretta will keep in the refrigerator for up to 3 days.
They do not freeze well.

SOFT CARAMEL PEARS

12 small dessert pears

6 oz/170 g caster sugar

2 tablespoons cornflour

5 fl oz/150 ml double cream

serves 6

1. Measure the sugar into a heavy saucepan, preferably stainless steel or copper.
Moisten with 4 fl oz/100 ml cold water, bring slowly to the boil, and caramelize to a dark red colour (10–12 mins).
Carefully add 2 pt/1 litre water and return to the boil.
2. Peel the pears whole, and leave their stalks on.
Remove the insides of the pears with a melon baller from the underside.
3. Poach the pears in the caramel syrup for 20–30 mins.
Remove from the hot syrup.
4. Dilute cornflour with 3 tablespoons cold water and stir into the boiling syrup to thicken slightly.
5. Stir in the cream and pour over pears.
Allow to cool and serve with vanilla ice cream.
Caramel Pears will keep for up to 3 days in the refrigerator or will freeze for 3 months without the cream.

DEVONSHIRE JUNKETS

Soft and smooth and served quite cold.
Originally junkets were made at the dairy as a nursery
pudding. The junkets have become very popular with grown-
ups too, especially those with a gentle stomach.

1 pt/600 ml full cream milk

1 tablespoon clear honey

2 fl oz/50 ml dark rum or coffee

1 tablespoon rennet essence

pinch fresh nutmeg

serves 4–5

1. Warm the milk over a basin of hot water
to a temperature of 37°C/98°F. No warmer.
Stir in the clear honey, flavouring and
rennet essence.
2. Pour into attractive stem glasses and leave
in a warm place to set. Setting will take
15–20 mins.
When the junkets have set, put them in the
refrigerator to chill.
Serve Devonshire Junkets very cold with a
grating of fresh nutmeg.
Vanilla or cinnamon junkets are an excellent
accompaniment to any poached fruit.

TUTTI FRUTTI YOGURT ICE

2 oz/50 g French candied peel

2 fl oz/50 ml Kirsch

4 oz/115 g icing sugar

1 pt/600 ml natural yogurt

serves 6

1. Finely chop the candied peel, and leave to
macerate in the Kirsch for 15–20 mins.
2. Blend the icing sugar into yogurt, and stir
in the fruit peel and Kirsch.
Freeze the yogurt ice in a metal basin for 60
mins. After this time whisk the yogurt to
break up any pieces of ice. Return to the
freezer and whisk every 20 mins until quite
firm. A further 1½ hrs.
If the yogurt ice becomes too hard leave it in
the refrigerator for 20 mins to soften.
To serve: Spoon into coupe dishes and offer
Langues des Chats biscuits as an
accompaniment (see page 88).
Tutti Frutti Yogurt Ice may be kept frozen for
up to 8 weeks.

SOUFFLÉ GLACÉ AU GRAND MARNIER

4 eggs (size 3)

3 tablespoons clear honey

3 fl oz/75 ml Grand Marnier

10 fl oz/300 ml double cream

orange (zest)

15 fl oz/450 ml natural yogurt

TO DECORATE:
2 oranges

2 oz/50 g dark covering chocolate

serves 6–8

1. Choose 6½ in/17 cm souflé dish. Cut a
piece of stiff card to fit neatly around the dish
to raise the edge by 2 in/5 cm.
2. Separate the eggs into two mixing bowls.
3. Measure 1 tablespoon of clear honey into
the yolks, add the Grand Marnier and whisk
until pale in colour. An electric mixer is best.
4. Measure 2 tablespoons of clear honey into
the egg whites and whisk until they form
soft peaks.
5. Loosely whip the cream, add finely grated
orange zest and stir in yogurt.
6. Fold yolks into egg whites and lastly fold
in yogurt and cream.
7. Pour the soufflé mixture into the prepared
dish and freeze for 3½–4 hrs. If the soufflé
becomes too hard, leave it to stand in the
refrigerator for 20 mins before serving.
To serve: Remove the stiff card and decorate
with rosettes of whipped cream, orange
segments and chocolate cut outs. To prepare
the chocolate cut outs: melt the covering
chocolate over a saucepan of hot water, and
allow to set on a piece of flat plastic sheeting.
Cut out the required shapes with a biscuit
cutter. For the special occasion spun sugar
(see page 6) is the perfect centre piece.
Freezes for up to 8 weeks.

Rhubarb and Ginger Yogurt Ice

RHUBARB AND GINGER YOGURT ICE

6 fl oz/175 ml orange juice
3 oz/85 g golden granulated sugar
1½ lb/700 g young rhubarb
½ oz/115 g stem ginger
10 fl oz/300 ml natural yogurt

TO DECORATE:
1 lime

1 bunch fresh mint

1 stick young rhubarb

1 piece stem ginger

serves 6
Adjust freezer to coldest setting.

1. Measure orange juice into a stainless steel saucepan.
Add the sugar, and bring to boil.
2. Peel the rhubarb, cut up finely, and poach in the syrup with the ginger for 8–10 mins.
3. Liquidize the fruit with the juices, rub through a fine sieve and leave to cool.
Blend in the yogurt and freeze in a metal basin for 60 mins.
After this time whisk the sorbet to break up any pieces of ice. Return to the freezer and whisk every 20 mins until quite firm, a further 1½ hrs.
If the sorbet becomes too hard, leave it in the refrigerator for 20 mins to soften before serving.
Serve on chilled plates. Shape the sorbet between two spoons dipped in warm water. Decorate with mint leaves, matchsticks of young rhubarb, stem ginger, and a twist of fresh lime. Offer Ginger lace Cones as an accompaniment (see page 89).
Rhubarb and Ginger Yogurt Ice will freeze for up to 8 weeks.

MAY

Riz à l'Imperatrice; Strawberry and Lime Syllabub;
Mousseline of Champagne Rhubarb;
Sour Cherry Pancakes with Kirsch and Cinnamon;
Flan Bourdalaise; Black Cherry Mousses with Yogurt;
Pineapple Baskets of Strawberries and Oranges; Puit d'Amour;
Schwarzwalder Torte; Apricot and Almond Streusel

RIZ À L'IMPERATRICE

Here, the silky smooth taste of ambrosia is set beneath a celestial cloud with a cordon of red jelly.

2 oz/50 ml short grain rice
1 pt/600 ml milk
¼ oz/8 g powdered gelatine
2 eggs, (size 3) separated
2 'oz/50 g candied fruit
2 fl oz/50 ml Kirsch
5 fl oz/150 ml natural yogurt
2 tablespoons golden granulated sugar

TO DECORATE:
1 tablet red jelly

serves 5–6

1. Make up the jelly using half the recommended amount of water.
Pour half the jelly into a 2 pt/1 litre jelly mould.
Set the remaining jelly in a small metal basin.
To prepare the rice:
2. Wash the rice in cold water, bring the milk to boil and cook rice over heat for 50–55 mins, stirring occasionally.
3. Soften the gelatine in 4 tablespoons cold water for 2–3 mins.
4. Separate the two egg yolks into a large basin. Reserve whites.
Pour the boiling rice over the eggs and add the softened gelatine. Allow the rice to cool completely.
5. Cut up the candied fruit and macerate in Kirsch for 10–15 mins.
6. Stir the yogurt into the setting rice followed by the fruit and Kirsch.
7. Whisk the egg whites together with the sugar until they form soft peaks.
8. Fold the beaten egg whites into now setting rice, pour into the prepared jelly mould and leave to set for 2½–3 hrs.

To serve:
Dip the jelly mould into warm water and release onto a large serving plate. Cut up the jelly and spread into an attractive border.
Riz à l'Imperatrice will keep in the refrigerator for up to 4 days. It does not freeze well.

STRAWBERRY AND LIME SYLLABUB

12 oz/350 g fresh strawberries
10 fl oz/300 ml double cream
2 tablespoons clear honey
4 limes
7 oz/200 g low fat soft cheese

serves 6

1. Reserve 6 of the best strawberries for decoration.
Purée the remaining fruit, and rub through a fine sieve to remove unwanted pips.
2. Loosely whip the cream with the honey, and blend in the soft cheese. Use your food mixer or processor for blending.
3. Finely grate the zest of 3 limes. Add zest and juice to the cheese, and blend in the strawberry purée.
4. Divide the syllabub between 6 stem glasses and chill for at least 1 hr before serving. Decorate with strawberries and slices of lime.
Offer Savoy Biscuits as an accompaniment (see page 89).
Strawberry and Lime Syllabubs will keep for up to 8 hrs in the refrigerator. Syllabubs do not freeze well.

MOUSSELINE OF CHAMPAGNE RHUBARB

A pretty little mousse bound with yogurt, cream and ginger.

1 lb/450 g pink champagne rhubarb
2 oz/50 g golden granulated sugar
½ oz/15 g stem ginger
2 tablespoons ginger syrup
2 teaspoons powdered gelatine
5 fl oz/150 ml double cream
5 fl oz/150 ml natural yogurt

TO DECORATE:
1 oz/25 g stem ginger
1 lime

serves 6

1. Reserve 1 stick of tender rhubarb for decoration.
Cut the remaining fruit into small pieces and place in a stainless steel saucepan. Add 3 fl oz/75 ml water with sugar, ginger and ginger syrup.
Simmer the rhubarb, covered, for 5–10 mins.
2. Purée the cooked rhubarb in a liquidizer and rub through a fine sieve to remove the stringy bits.
3. Soften the gelatine in 2 tablespoons cold water, 2–3 mins, and then dissolve into the hot purée and allow to cool.
4. Loosely whip the cream and blend in the yogurt.
When the rhubarb is just setting, carefully fold in the yogurt and cream.
5. Pour the mousse into 6 attractive glasses and leave to set for 1½–2 hrs.
To decorate:
6. Peel the rhubarb, cut into 1 in/2.5 cm lengths and cut the lengths, into thin matchsticks.
Cut the stem ginger into the same sized strips.
Thinly slice the lime and make a cut into each slice, as if to mark half past six.
7. Arrange the fine garnish over each mousse and serve with Savoy Biscuits (see page 89).
Champagne Rhubarb Mousseline will keep in the refrigerator for up to 3 days. It does not freeze well.

SOUR CHERRY PANCAKES WITH KIRSCH AND CINNAMON

A tempting and original way to serve early season cherries, bound in a yogurt sauce, wrapped in wafer-thin pancakes. Simply delicious.

3 oz/85 g golden granulated sugar
½ pt/300 ml water
1 cinnamon stick
12 oz/350 g sour cherries
1 × recipe Pancakes (see page 16)

FILLING:
2 tablespoons cornflour
4 tablespoons cold water
5 fl oz/150 ml natural yogurt
2 egg yolks
2 tablespoons golden granulated sugar
5 fl oz/150 ml milk
2 tablespoons Kirsch

serves 6
Preheat oven 350°F/180°C/gas mark 4.

1. Prepare a syrup from sugar and water, add the cinnamon and simmer for 3–4 mins.
2. Stone the cherries with a cherry stoner and poach them in the syrup for 8–10 mins.
To prepare the filling:
3. Dilute the cornflour with cold water. Blend into the yogurt and stir in the egg yolks and sugar.
4. Bring the milk to boil and whisk into the yogurt.
Return to the heat and stir back to boil.
5. Drain the cherries and bind them together with some of the sauce, you may not need it all. Add a little Kirsch to taste.
6. Lay the pancakes out in rows. Put a spoonful of cherries onto each pancake, roll up neatly and arrange in an ovenproof dish. Cover the dish with foil and warm in the oven 15–20 mins. Serve Sour Cherry Pancakes with vanilla ice cream or pouring cream.
The dish may be frozen for up to 3 weeks.

FLAN BOURDALAISE

A beautiful combination of apples, apricots and fine cinnamon displayed in a picture-like flan.

12 oz/350 g Hazelnut and Cinnamon Pastry (see page 92).

12 oz/350 g dessert apples

12 oz/350 g fresh apricots

½ lemon (juice)

½ teaspoon ground cinnamon

pinch ground cloves

1 tablespoon soft brown sugar

TO DECORATE:
2 oz/50 g apricot preserve

serves 6
Preheat oven 375°F/190°C/gas mark 5

1. Grease and line an 8 in/20 cm flan ring with hazelnut pastry.
Half bake the flan blind for 15–20 mins.
2. Reserve 1 apple and 7 whole apricots for decoration.
Peel, core and slice the remaining apples and cook, covered, together with apricots, lemon juice, cinnamon, and cloves until quite soft. About 8–10 mins.
Add the sugar to sweeten and spread into the half-baked flan case.
3. Cut the apricots into quarters, and arrange them standing up around the edge of the flan.
4. Remove the core from the apple, leave the skin on and slice thinly.
Arrange the apple slices in the centre overlapping neatly.
5. Return the flan to the oven (middle shelf) for a further 20 mins,
To glaze the flan:
6. Dilute the apricot preserve with 1 tablespoon water, bring to the boil and glaze flan thinly with a flat brush.
Serve Flan Bourdalaise warm or cold with vanilla ice cream as a lunchtime dessert.

BLACK CHERRY MOUSSES WITH YOGURT

First class black cherries are imported from Spain in May. They have an excellent flavour and are used to create this impressive mousseline.

4 fl oz/100 ml red wine

3 tablespoons golden granulated sugar

1 cinnamon stick

1 lb/450 g black cherries (stoned)

2 teaspoons powdered gelatine

5 fl oz/150 ml double cream

5 fl oz/150 ml natural yogurt

TO DECORATE:
3 oz/85 g dark chocolate

12 cherries (with stalks)

5 fl oz/150 ml whipped cream

serves 6

1. Prepare a syrup from the red wine and sugar.
Add the cinnamon and simmer the stoned cherries for 8–10 mins.
2. Soften the powdered gelatine in 2 tablespoons cold water for 2–3 mins.
3. Purée the cherries with their syrup in a liquidizer.
Dissolve the gelatine into the warm purée and allow to cool.
4. Loosely whip the cream, and blend in the yogurt.
Carefully fold the cream into the setting purée.
5. Pour the mixture into 6 attractive glasses and chill in the refrigerator for 1½–2 hrs.
6. Decorate each mousse with flakes of chocolate, a rosette of whipped cream and 2 cherries.
Black Cherry Mousses will keep in the refrigerator for 2–3 days.

Pineapple Basket of Strawberries and Oranges

PINEAPPLE BASKETS OF STRAWBERRIES AND ORANGES

A refreshing idea for cocktail parties.

2 small pineapples
4 oranges
8 oz/225 g strawberries
3 fl oz/75 ml dark rum

serves 4

1. Cut the pineapples in half from top to bottom.
Remove the central core, and loosen the flesh with a grapefruit knife.

Cut the pineapple flesh into even sized pieces and moisten with dark rum. If necessary sweeten with a little soft sugar.
2. Segment the oranges. Halve the strawberries and leave all three fruits to macerate in the rum.
3. Refrigerate for 1½–2 hrs, the longer the better.
To serve:
Fill each pineapple half with the fruits and set each onto crushed ice.

Schwarzwalder Torte
Recipe on page 38

PUIT D'AMOUR

Roughly translated it means the Well of Love.
Hidden in this well of velvety yogurt cream are the first of
the season's strawberries.

1 × recipe Quark Flaky Pastry (see page 91).

8 oz/225 g new English strawberries

2 oz/50 g strawberry jam.

FILLING:
2 tablespoons cornflour

5 fl oz/150 ml natural yogurt

2 eggs (size 3) separated

5 fl oz/150 ml milk

2 drops vanilla essence

2 tablespoons golden granulated sugar

serves 6
Preheat oven 375°F/190°C/gas mark 5

1. Lightly grease an 8 in/20 cm flan ring, and thinly line with flaky pastry.
Rest for 40 mins and bake blind for 25–30 mins.
2. Spread the strawberry jam into the flan base and sprinkle the strawberries over, reserving one for decoration.
To prepare the filling:
3. Dilute cornflour with 4 tablespoons cold water.
Blend with the yogurt and stir in egg yolks.
4. Bring the milk to boil with vanilla essence. Whisk the boiling milk into the yogurt and return to the saucepan.
Stir back to boil and allow to thicken.
5. Whisk egg whites with sugar until they form soft peaks.
Carefully fold in the beaten egg whites with a large metal spoon.
6. Spread the filling into the flan case, set in the refrigerator and decorate with a single strawberry. Will keep for up to 3 days. Does not freeze well.

SCHWARZWALDER TORTE

The Black Forests of Southern Germany have inspired this composition of black cherries, Kirsch, dark chocolate and cream. The chocolate flakes imitate the carpet of pine needles found deep in the forest.

Illustrated on page 37

1 × recipe Rich Dark Chocolate Sponge (see page 94).

FILLING:
2 oz/50 g golden granulated sugar

½ pt/300 ml boiling water

1 cinnamon stick

1 lb/450 g bitter dark cherries

2 tablespoons cornflour

KIRSCH FILLING:
12 fl oz/350 ml double cream

1 tablespoon fine sugar

2 tablespoons Kirsch

5 fl oz/150 ml natural yogurt

TO DECORATE:
6 oz/170 g plain dark chocolate

10 whole cherries (with stalks)

1 tablespoon icing sugar

10 fl oz/300 ml light syrup (made with 2 oz/50 g golden granulated sugar).

serves 8–10

1. Dissolve 2 oz/50 g golden granulated sugar into boiling water.
2. Add the cinnamon and simmer for 3–4 mins.
Reserve 10 cherries for decoration.
Stone the remaining cherries, and poach them in the syrup for 8–10 mins.
Remove the cherries from the syrup, and thicken with cornflour diluted with 4 tablespoons cold water.
Return syrup to boil to thicken, add the cherries, and leave to cool.
3. Dip the reserved 10 cherries into the thickened syrup and leave to one side.
4. Loosely whip the cream with the fine sugar and Kirsch.
Blend in the yogurt to make a smooth cream filling.
5. Slice the chocolate sponge into 3 with a serrated knife.
Moisten each layer of sponge with light syrup and sprinkle with Kirsch.
Put the bottom layer of sponge onto a round cake or flan base.

Pipe the prepared Kirsch filling into concentric rings over the first layer.
Distribute the cherries between the rings of cream. Sandwich the second layer of sponge and repeat the process.
6. Cover the entire gâteau with a thin layer of cream.
Soften the chocolate slightly in a warm place and scrape into chocolate curls. Save the curls for the centre decoration.
Refrigerate the remaining chocolate and grate finely. Cover the entire surface with grated chocolate and arrange a flower decoration in the centre.
Pipe 10 rosettes of whipped cream and top with 10 whole cherries, and dust lightly with icing sugar.
Chill Schwarzwalder Torte well before serving. Will keep for up to 3 days. This gâteau does not freeze well.

APRICOT AND ALMOND STREUSEL

1½ lb/675 g fresh apricots

2 tablespoons golden granulated sugar

STREUSEL TOPPING:
2 oz/50 g ground almonds

3 tablespoons whole meal flour

2 oz/50 g firm butter

2 oz/50 g golden granulated sugar

serves 4–5
Preheat oven 375°F/190°C/gas mark 5

1. Halve the apricots, and put them into a 2 pt/1 litre gratin dish. Add 3 tablespoons water and the sugar.
To prepare the streusel topping:
2. Rub all the dry ingredients together with the butter to form a crumb consistency. Use a food mixer on the slowest speed or food processor for 1 min.
3. Sprinkle the almond streusel over the prepared apricots and bake in centre oven for 45–50 mins.
Serve Apricot and Almond Streusel warm with pouring cream or with a smooth custard sauce.
Apricot and Almond Streusel will freeze for up to 8 weeks before baking.

JUNE

Strawberry Shortcake with Almonds;
English Strawberry Flan with Yogurt;
Blanc Manger aux Abricots; Strawberries Romanoff;
Poached Gooseberries with Sherry and Elderflower;
Apricot Jalousie; Gooseberry and Orange Sorbet;
Ice Strawberry Soufflé with Orange; Kentish Cherry Pie;
Pasta al Albicocco; Kiwi and Gooseberry Fool

Strawberry Shortcake with Almonds

A variation of a classical favourite.

THE SPONGE:

4 eggs (size 3) at room temperature

6 oz/170 g golden granulated sugar

6 oz/170 g whole meal flour

4 oz/115 g ground almonds

3 oz/85 g melted butter

FILLING:

1½ lb/675 g English strawberries

10 fl oz/300 ml double cream

1 teaspoon clear honey

TO DECORATE:

5 fl oz/150 ml double cream (whipped)

2 oz/50 g dark chocolate

serves 8
Preheat oven 375°F–190°C/gas mark 5

1. Line two baking sheets with greaseproof paper, mark three 7 in/18 cm circles with a pencil and leave to one side.
2. Melt the butter over a gentle heat, and leave at the back of the stove.
3. Separate 2 eggs into 2 mixing bowls, add 2 whole eggs to the egg yolks, and whisk together with ½ the sugar until a thick ribbon can be drawn across the surface.

4. Whisk egg whites together with the remaining sugar until soft peaks are formed. Fold the beaten egg whites into yolks with a large metal spoon.
5. Sieve the flours and ground almonds over the eggs and fold in as above.
Carefully fold in the melted butter and spoon the mixture into a piping bag fitted with ½ in/12 cm nozzle.
Pipe the mixture into spirals starting in the centre of each marked circle.
6. Bake the sponges for 25–30 mins.
To prepare the filling:
7. Choose 8 of the best strawberries for decoration.
Purée 6 oz/175 g of the strawberries in a liquidizer or rub them through a fine sieve.
8. Loosely whip the cream with honey and blend with the strawberry purée to a smooth cream.
To assemble;
9. Trim the three sponges into 7 in/18 cm circles. Save the trimmings for decoration.
10. Spread a thin layer of strawberry filling onto the first sponge. Scatter with ½ of the remaining strawberries and continue to build the layers, turning the final layer upside-down.
11. Rub the sponge trimmings through a fine sieve and use the crumbs to mask the sides of the shortcake.
To decorate:
12. Pipe 8 rosettes of whipped cream around the edge and decorate with 8 whole strawberries and 8 pieces of chocolate.
Strawberry Shortcake will keep in the refrigerator for up to 3 days or will freeze for up to 6 weeks.

ENGLISH STRAWBERRY FLAN WITH YOGURT

Strawberries and yogurt have earned themselves quite a reputation. Here is a delicious flan of strawberries set on a smooth yogurt cream.

1 × recipe Whole Meal Biscuit Pastry (see page 91)

1½ lb/675 g English strawberries

FILLING:
2 egg yolks

5 fl oz/150 ml natural yogurt

1 tablespoon golden granulated sugar

2 level tablespoons cornflour

zest of 1 orange

5 fl oz/150 ml milk

TO DECORATE:
3 oz/85 g strawberry preserve

serves 5–6
Preheat oven 400°F/205°C/gas mark 6

1. Lightly grease an 8 in/20 cm flan ring and line with biscuit pastry.
Leave to rest for 20 mins and bake blind for 25–30 mins.
To make the filling:
2. Separate the egg yolks into a basin, add yogurt, and stir in sugar. Dilute the cornflour with 3 tablespoons cold water and stir into the yogurt.
3. Finely grate the orange zest into the milk, bring to boil and pour over the yogurt.
Return the mixture to the saucepan, and stir back to boil.
Cover the yogurt cream with a butter paper and leave to cool.
To assemble:
4. Spread an even layer of yogurt cream into the bottom of the pre-baked flan case, and arrange the whole strawberries so that they completely cover the filling.
To glaze:
5. Dilute the strawberry preserve with 1 tablespoon water, bring to boil and glaze thinly with a flat brush.
Serve Strawberry Yogurt Flan quite cold as a lunch or dinner dessert. The flan will keep for up to 24 hrs when assembled. The flan case may be kept in a biscuit tin uncooked for 3–4 days or will freeze for up to 6 weeks. The same applies for the yogurt filling.

BLANCMANGER AUX ABRICOTS

A delicate mousseline of almonds, apricots, and fresh vanilla.

10 fl oz/300 ml milk

3 oz/85 g white marzipan

1 fresh vanilla pod

2 teaspoons powdered gelatine

3 tablespoons golden granulated sugar

2 tablespoons cold water

1 lb/450 g fresh apricots

5 fl oz/150 ml double cream

5 fl oz/150 ml natural yogurt

TO DECORATE:
5 fl oz/150 ml whipped cream

2 oz/50 g plain dark chocolate

serves 8

1. Measure milk into a saucepan with the marzipan and split vanilla pod. Bring to boil and dissolve the marzipan.
2. Soften the powdered gelatine in cold water for 2–3 mins.
3. Remove the milk from heat, stir in the softened gelatine and leave to cool.
4. Prepare a syrup from sugar and water.
5. Halve the apricots, and simmer in the syrup for 3–4 mins.
Take out 12 apricot halves, cut them into small pieces and put them in a small basin. Purée the remaining fruit in a liquidizer, or rub through a fine sieve. Adjust the consistency with syrup to that of single cream.
6. Moisten the apricot pieces with 2 tablespoons of purée. Divide the pieces between 8 stem glasses, and put to one side.
To prepare the mousseline:
7. Loosely whip the cream, and blend in the yogurt. Fold the cream into the setting milk, marzipan and vanilla.
8. Pour the mousseline into the prepared glasses and leave in the refrigerator to set, 1½–2 hrs.
To decorate:
9. Pipe a rosette of whipped cream in the centre of each mousse. Pour some apricot purée over the surface and decorate with a small piece of chocolate.
Blancmanger aux Abricots will keep in the refrigerator for up to 3 days.

Strawberries Romanoff

STRAWBERRIES ROMANOFF

The best English strawberries, the finest French Grand Marnier, and a ruby red port of Portugal, rendezvous beneath a sauce of strawberries and yogurt cream. Cèst lá saison Extra!

1½ lb/675 g English strawberries

10 fl oz/300 ml yogurt (strained see page 49) or lightly whipped double cream

12 fl oz/350 g fresh orange juice

5 fl oz/150 ml ruby port

3 fl oz/75 ml Grand Marnier

1 tablespoon icing sugar

TO DECORATE:
pistachio nuts or sprigs of fresh mint.

serves 4–5

1. Wash the strawberries, and remove stalks. Purée 6 oz/175 g of the largest fruits, and rub them through a fine sieve.
2. Blend the purée with the strained yogurt. Add 2 tablespoons port, 1 tablespoon Grand Marnier, and sweeten with a little icing sugar to taste. Keep the sauce in the refrigerator until needed.
3. Put the remaining strawberries in the orange juice, add the remaining port and Grand Marnier. Sweeten slightly with a little icing sugar. Allow the strawberries to macerate for at least 2 hrs before serving.
To serve:
4. Take the strawberries out of the liquid and arrange them in a glass bowl. Pour the sauce over the top and decorate with slices of strawberry, and a few mint leaves or pistachio nuts.

POACHED GOOSEBERRIES WITH SHERRY AND ELDERFLOWER

A simple and most effective dessert for any occasion.

3 oz/85 g golden granulated sugar
15 fl oz/450 ml water
1 orange (zest)
1 good head of elderflower
1 glass/150 ml medium sherry
1½ lb/675 g English gooseberries

TO SERVE:
1 fl oz/300 ml natural yogurt
2 oz/50 g dark elderberries

serves 6

1. Prepare a mild syrup from sugar and water.
2. Remove the zest from the orange with a vegetable peeler, cut the peel into thin strips and throw into the syrup with the elderflower and sherry. Simmer 10 mins.
3. Top and tail the gooseberries with a sharp knife, and poach fruit in the boiling syrup for no longer than 2 mins. Please watch them carefully, gooseberries cook very quickly. As soon as they become soft green in colour they are cooked. Few people enjoy mushy goosberries.
Leave the gooseberries to cool in their own juices and chill well before serving.
To serve:
4. Arrange the gooseberries in a neat pile on large white plates and decorate with ripe elderberries.
5. Stir some natural yogurt and serve to one side.
Poached Gooseberries will keep for up to 4 days in the refrigerator. They may be frozen for 2–3 months.

APRICOT JALOUSIE

Jalousie is the old French word for a slatted blind. This delicate pastry represents the shutters opening to reveal moist little apricots resting on a fine almond sponge.

8 oz/225 g Puff Pastry (see page 90)
8 oz/225 g fresh apricots
2 oz/50 g apricot preserve
1 × recipe Fine Almond Sponge (see page 94)

TO GLAZE:
1 tablespoon icing sugar egg, beaten

serves 6
Preheat oven 400°F/205°C/gas mark 6

1. Roll out puff pastry into a rectangle 10 × 8 in/25 × 20 cm. Cut the rectangle in half down the middle.
Fold the first strip down the middle, making sure there is plenty of flour between the fold. Make a series of even cuts into the pastry ⅔ way towards the open edge, forming vents when opened out.
Leave the pastry to rest in the refrigerator while you make the almond sponge filling.
To assemble:
2. Spread a thin layer of apricot preserve onto the un-cut piece of puff pastry. Lay the strip of pastry onto a baking sheet and pipe or spread the almond filling to within 1 in/25 cm of the edge.
3. Halve the apricots, and position them over the filling.
4. Moisten the edges with beaten egg, and lay the vented piece of pastry over the top, sealing the edges firmly.
Brush the entire pastry with beaten egg; a good pinch of salt will improve the final glaze.
5. Bake the Jalousie near the top of oven for 40–50 mins.
6. To finish, dust with icing sugar and return to the top shelf of oven until the sugar has lightly caramelized (2–3 mins).
Serve Apricot Jalousie warm with vanilla ice cream or cold as a tea fancy.
Jalousie will keep for up to 3 days in a biscuit tin but is best eaten the day made. May be frozen before baking for up to 6 weeks.

GOOSEBERRY AND ORANGE SORBET

The sweetest of our English gooseberries appear on the market in June. A delicious way of presenting them to your guests is to freeze them into a mouth watering sorbet with a hint of fresh orange.

1½ lb/675 g English gooseberries

5 oz/140 g golden granulated sugar

8 fl oz/250 ml unsweetened orange juice

1 tablespoon orange flower water

TO DECORATE:
3 oranges

6 mint leaves

serves 6
Adjust freezer to coldest setting.

1. Top and tail the gooseberries with a sharp knife.
2. Dissolve the sugar into the orange juice, add orange flower water and bring to boil. Throw the gooseberries into the boiling syrup and simmer gently for not longer than 2 mins. After this time take out 12 whole fruits and reserve for decoration.
Continue to cook the gooseberries until they fall apart, 4–5 mins. Liquidize the gooseberries in their juices and leave to cool completely.
3. Pour the purée into a metal bowl, and freeze for 60 mins. After this time whisk the sorbet to remove any lumps of ice. Return the sorbet to the freezer and whisk every 20 mins until quite smooth. (A further 1½ hrs). If the sorbet becomes too hard, leave it in the refrigerator to soften for 20 mins.
To serve:
4. Shape the sorbet between 2 tablepoons dipped into warm water. Arrange on a dessert plate and decorate with segments of orange two poached gooseberries and a sprig of fresh mint.

ICED STRAWBERRY SOUFFLÉ WITH ORANGE

1 lb/450 g English strawberries

3 tablespoons orange blossom honey

3 oz/85 g golden granulated sugar

3 egg whites (size 3)

10 fl oz/300 ml double cream

10 fl oz/300 ml natural yogurt

2 fl oz/50 ml orange liqueur

1 orange (zest)

TO DECORATE:
5 fl oz/150 ml whipping cream

1 orange

spun sugar (see page 6)

serves 8

1. Choose a 6½ in/17 cm soufflé dish. Cut a piece of stiff card to raise the edge of the dish by 2 in/5 cm and sellotape in position.
2. Reserve 8 of the best strawberries for decoration.
Purée the remaining fruit, and rub through a fine sieve to remove the pips.
3. Measure the honey into a stainless steel or copper saucepan.
Warm the honey over a gentle heat, add the sugar and boil steadily for 2 mins.
4. Whisk the egg whites to form soft peaks and gradually pour the boiling sugar over the whites. Continue whisking until the egg whites form stiff peaks.
5. Loosely whip the cream, fold in the yogurt and add the orange liqueur and the finely grated zest of orange.
Blend in the strawberry purée, and fold in the beaten egg whites.
Pour the mixture into the prepare soufflé dish and freeze for at least 4 hrs.
If the soufflé becomes too firm, leave it in the refrigerator to soften slightly, 20–25 mins, or microwave briefly.
6. Decorate with rosettes of whipped cream, orange segments, strawberries and spun sugar.

Pasta al Albicocco

KENTISH CHERRY PIE

8 oz/225 g Quark Flaky Pastry (see page 91)
2 lb/900 g dark cherries (stoned)
7 fl oz/200 ml full bodied red wine
3 oz/85 g golden granulated sugar
1 cinnamon stick
1 small bay leaf

TO GLAZE:
1 egg, beaten with a pinch of salt

serves 5–6
Preheat oven 400°F/205°c/gas mark 6

1. Place cherries in a 2 pt/1 litre pie dish. Pour over the red wine, add sugar, cinnamon, and bay leaf.
2. Roll the pastry out on a floured surface to a thickness of $\frac{1}{8}$in/3 mm. Cut two 1 in/2.5 cm wide strips of pastry, brush the edges of the pie dish with beaten egg and salt, and stretch the lengths of pastry around the dish.
Brush the edges once more with beaten egg, and cover entirely with the remaining pastry. Cut out 5–6 leaves for decoration, glaze with beaten egg, and rest for at least 1 hr.
3. Bake the cherry pie in centre oven for 60 mins.
Serve Kentish Cherry Pie with lightly whipped cream.
The pie may be frozen for up to 8 weeks before baking.

PASTA AL ALBICOCCO

5 oz/140 g pasta spirals

2 pt/1.1 litre water

3 tablespoons orange blossom honey

APRICOT ZABAGLIONE:
2 egg yolks

2 tablespoons apricot brandy

TO DECORATE:
6 (1 small tin) apricots

1 oz/25 g pistachio nuts (blanched in boiling
    water 3–4 mins)

6 Almond Tuile biscuits (see page 89)

serves 6

1. Dissolve honey in water, bring to the boil
and remove any resulting foam.
Simmer the pasta in the mild honey syrup
for 10–12 mins.
(If the pasta is not required immediately, it is
a good idea to keep it in cold water until
needed.) Reserve the honey syrup for
reheating later.
2. Cut the apricots into thin slices, toast the
almonds lightly, and peel the pistachio nuts.
Lastly put 6 dessert plates to warm. At this
stage you are free to join your guests at the
table.
When the dessert is required, put the pasta
back into the syrup and warm gently.
To prepare the apricot zabaglione:
3. Put the egg yolks into a mixing bowl and
whisk over a hot water bath with the apricot
brandy, 2–3 mins with an electric mixer.
4. Drain the pasta well, add the sliced
apricots and fold in the apricot zabaglione.
Put a spoonful of the warm pasta onto each
plate, sprinkle with pistachio nuts, and serve
with almond biscuits.

KIWI AND GOOSEBERRY FOOL
Quick and easy, any fool can make it.

2 oz/50 g golden granulated sugar

½ pt/300 ml water

1½ lb/700 g gooseberries

1 teaspoon powdered gelatine

5 fl oz/150 ml double cream

5 fl oz/150 ml natural yogurt

3 kiwi fruits

serves 6

1. Prepare a light syrup from sugar and
water.
Poach the gooseberries in the syrup for 2–3
mins.
Reserve 12 good looking gooseberries for
decoration.
Continue cooking the remaining fruit until
they fall apart.
2. Soften the powdered gelatine in 2
tablespoons cold water (2–3 mins).
3. Liquidize the gooseberries, stir in the
softened gelatine and leave to cool
completely.
4. Loosely whip cream, and blend in yogurt.
5. Peel 2 kiwi fruit, cut into even pieces and
stir into the yogurt cream.
6. Fold the cream into the setting gooseberry
purée and pour into 6 serving glasses.
7. Leave the fools in the refrigerator for 1½–2
hrs to set.
Decorate each glass with two poached
gooseberries and a slice of the remaining
kiwi fruit.
This particular fool will keep for up to 3 days
in the refrigerator. It freezes reasonably well,
6–8 weeks.

JULY

Strawberry Yogurt Ice;
Black Cherry Compote with Kirsch and Cinnamon;
Scarlet Blancmange; Evening Swans; Pêches Maintenon;
Champagne Sorbet; Carousel des Fruits; July Pancakes;
Pêches Rafraîchis Bourguignonne; Raspberry Tulips;
Pêches Cardinal; Watermelon Fruit Basket.

STRAWBERRY YOGURT ICE

Strawberry Yogurt Ice can be served as an evening dessert with a delicate orange sauce, or as a simple teatime treat.

10 oz/285 g English strawberries
2 oz/50 g icing sugar
1 tablespoon lemon juice
3 tablespoons Grand Marnier (optional)
10 fl oz/300 ml natural yogurt
ORANGE SAUCE: *4 large oranges*
1 tablespoon soft brown sugar
2 teaspoons cornflour
3 tablespoons Grand Marnier

serves 5–6

1. Reserve 6 perfect strawberries for decoration.
Purée the remaining fruit and rub through a fine sieve to remove the pips.
2. Add the icing sugar, lemon juice and Grand Marnier.
3. Blend in the strawberry purée, and freeze in a metal basin for 60 mins. Whisk the yogurt ice every 20 mins to break up any pieces of ice for further 1½ hrs. If the yogurt ice becomes too firm, leave to soften in the refrigerator for 20 mins, or microwave briefly.
To prepare the orange sauce:
4. Remove the zest from the oranges with a citrus zester. Throw the zest into a saucepan of boiling water to soften, 2–3 mins.
5. Squeeze the juice into a stainless steel saucepan, add the sugar and bring to the boil.
6. Dilute cornflour with 2 tablespoons cold water and stir into the boiling juice a little at a time. When the sauce reaches the consistency of single cream add the orange zest and Grand Marnier.

To serve:
7. Shape the yogurt ice between two tablespoons dipped into warm water. These shapes can be made well before the meal and kept on greaseproof paper in the freezer. Arrange the shapes onto chilled plates, pour around the orange sauce, and decorate with a whole strawberry.
Offer Langues des Chats or Tuille Biscuits (see page 88).
Try replacing strawberries with other soft berry fruits; raspberries, peaches, cherries, blackcurrants and mango ...

BLACK CHERRY COMPOTE WITH KIRSCH AND CINNAMON

1½ lb/675 g dark cherries (stoned)
3 oz/85 g soft brown sugar
1 cinnamon stick
2 teaspoons cornflour
2 fl oz/50 ml Kirsch
TO SERVE: *10 fl oz/300 ml natural yogurt*

serves 4–5

1. Prepare a light syrup from 1 pt/600 ml of water and the sugar.
Add the prepared cherries, and simmer with the cinnamon for 10–12 mins.
2. Dilute the cornflour in 4 tablespoons cold water, add to the syrup and return to boil to thicken. Add the Kirsch, and leave to cool. The cherries are now ready to serve, although if kept overnight in the refrigerator their flavour will be greatly improved. Serve warm or cold with natural yogurt.
Black Cherry Compote will keep in the refrigerator for up to 3 days or will freeze for 3 months.

SCARLET BLANCMANGE

Tickle the palate with this sumptuous collection of red berry fruits bound in a velvet dream.

1 lb/450 g fresh raspberries
6 oz/170 g blackcurrants
12 oz/350 g redcurrants
15 fl oz/450 ml water
2 oz/50 g golden granulated sugar
2 level tablespoons cornflour
2 egg whites
2 tablespoons golden granulated sugar

TO DECORATE:
5 fl oz/150 ml natural yogurt

serves 6

1. Wash and prepare soft fruits.
Reserve 6 oz/175 g raspberries and 6 small bunches of currants.
Put the remaining fruit into a stainless steel saucepan with the sugar and water. Simmer for 8–10 mins.
2. Purée the fruit with the syrup, rub through a fine sieve, and return to the saucepan. Reserve 3 tablespoons of the purée at this stage for decoration.
3. Dilute cornflour in 6 tablespoons cold water.
Add the cornflour to the purée and return to the boil to thicken.
4. Whisk the egg whites with 2 tablespoons sugar until they form soft peaks.
Carefully fold the beaten egg whites into hot thickened purée, add the reserved raspberries, and pour into 6 stem glasses or one large serving dish. Allow to chill for 60 mins.
To decorate:
5. Stir the yogurt and pour over the surface of the blancmange.
Spoon a trail of the reserved purée through the yogurt and make a simple swirl on the surface.
Decorate with a small bunch of currants dipped into egg white and then into caster sugar.
Scarlet Blancmange will keep for up to 4 days in the refrigerator or may be frozen for 6–8 weeks.
Other soft fruits can be used instead of those mentioned, although I would advise you retain the blackcurrants for their excellent flavour.

EVENING SWANS

A graceful way to present soft summer fruits before your evening guests.

1 × recipe Choux Pastry (see page 92)
beaten egg
1 × recipe Strawberry Yogurt Ice (see page 46)
1 lb/450 g fresh raspberries
5 fl oz/150 ml natural yogurt
2 oz/50 g plain covering chocolate

serves 6
Preheat oven 400°F/205°C/gas mark 6

1. Lightly grease 2 baking sheets or line with non stick paper.
Spoon or pipe the pastry into 12 heaps no bigger than a walnut, 2 finger widths apart.
2. Put the remaining choux pastry into a large paper cornet.
Cut $\frac{1}{4}$ in/6 mm off the end, and pipe out 12 swan necks on a separate baking sheet. (Extra bodies and necks are useful frozen for later use, 6–8 weeks).
3. Brush the bodies and the necks with beaten egg, and bake near the top of the oven. The necks will take 10–15 mins to cook, the bodies at least 40 mins.
4. Split the choux buns in half with a sharp knife, cut the upper half in two to form the wings and leave to cool.
5. Put a ball of yogurt ice into each swan. Arrange the two wings in position, and keep in the freezer until needed.
6. Melt the chocolate over a saucepan of hot water or microwave for about 60 secs.
Dip the faces of the swans in the chocolate, and leave to set on greaseproof paper.
7. Purée the remaining fruit and rub through a fine sieve to remove the pips. Sweeten with a little icing sugar to taste and leave to one side.
To assemble:
8. Spoon the raspberry purée onto 6 large dessert plates.
Position a neck for each swan, and arrange two swans per plate.
Feather a small amount of yogurt through the raspberry purée to suggest movement. Serve immediately.

PÊCHES MAINTENON

Everyone has their favourite dessert, this is one of mine, the peaches, the raspberries, the Kirsch, the yogurt and the fresh vanilla. A perfect balance of natural flavours, very attractive in tall stem glasses.

FRUIT:
3 large peaches

12 oz/350 g fresh raspberries

1 tablespoon golden granulated sugar

6–8 Savoy Biscuits (see page 89)

3 tablespoons Kirsch

MOUSSE:
5 fl oz/150 ml natural yogurt

5 fl oz/150 ml double cream

1 tablespoon golden granulated sugar

½ fresh vanilla pod

2 egg whites

2 teaspoons powdered gelatine

TO DECORATE:
5 fl oz/150 ml whipping cream

6–8 crystallized mimosa flowers

serves 6–8

1. Reserve 6–8 perfect raspberries for decoration.
Purée the remaining fruit with the sugar, and rub through a fine sieve to remove any pips. Add Kirsch and leave to one side.
2. Throw the peaches into boiling water to loosen their skins, 2–3 mins.
Slice the fruit thinly and distribute between 6–8 serving glasses.
3. Crumble a Savoy Biscuit into each glass and moisten with a little raspberry purée.
To prepare the mousse:
4. Soften the powdered gelatine in 2 tablespoons cold water, 2–3 mins, and melt over a saucepan of boiling water.
5. Loosely whip the cream and blend in the yogurt.
6. Split open the fresh vanilla pod, scrape out the tiny black seeds and disperse in the sugar.
7. Whisk the egg whites with the sugar to form soft peaks.
8. Stir the melted gelatine into the cream and yogurt and fold in the beaten egg whites with a large metal spoon.

Pour the mousse into the prepared glasses, and leave to set in the refrigerator for 1½–2 hrs.
To decorate:
9. Pipe a neat rosette onto each mousse and pour around the raspberry purée. Decorate with an upturned raspberry and a mimosa flower.
Pêche Maintenon will keep in the refrigerator for up to 2 days.

CHAMPAGNE SORBET

Champagne Sorbet is designed to impress on those special occasions when no expenses are spared. Considered by many to be the ultimate sensation in frozen desserts, Champagne Sorbet deserves the attention of a king.

1 bottle/750 ml dry champagne

10 fl oz/300 ml water

11 oz/325 g golden granulated sugar

2 large oranges

6 strawberries

serves 6
Adjust your freezer to coldest setting.

1. Prepare a syrup from the sugar and water, add the finely grated zest and the juice of the orange.
Simmer for 10–12 mins, add the champagne, strain through a fine sieve and leave to cool over ice.
2. Freeze the sorbet in a metal basin for 60 mins, after this time whisk the sorbet to break up any pieces of ice.
Return to the freezer and whisk every 20 mins until quite firm. (A further 1½ hrs).
If the sorbet should become too firm, allow to soften in the refrigerator 20 mins or transfer to a plastic basin and a brief encounter in a microwave will have the same effect.
3. Serve the sorbet in chilled champagne glasses, and decorate with segments of fresh orange and a whole strawberry.
Offer Savoy Biscuits as an accompaniment (see page 89).
Champagne Sorbet is best enjoyed on the day of making.

CAROUSEL DES FRUITS

*A featherlight ring of choux pastry filled with yogurt cream
and soft summer fruits.*

5 fl oz/150 ml natural yogurt
1 × recipe Choux Pastry (see page 92)
5 fl oz/150 ml double cream
1 tablespoon clear honey
1 lb/450 g summer fruits
TO GLAZE: *3 oz/85 g redcurrant jelly*

serves 6
Preheat oven 400°F/205°C/gas mark 6

1. Put the yogurt into a coffee filter or muslin and leave to drain for 60 mins.
2. Lightly grease an 8 in/20 cm flan ring and set onto a baking sheet.
3. Put the choux pastry into a piping bag fitted with a large, plain ½ in/12 mm nozzle. Pipe the choux pastry inside the prepared flan ring.
Bake the ring near the top of the oven for 40–45 mins. Please allow the pastry to dry out properly in the oven.
To assemble:
4. Loosely whip the cream with honey, and blend with the strained yogurt.
5. Slice the pastry ring in half, and remove any uncooked pastry.
Spread a layer of the yogurt cream into the bottom half.
Invert the second half over the first and fill again with cream.
Prepare the soft fruit and decorate, entirely covering the filling.
To glaze:
6. Soften the redcurrant jelly over a slow heat and glaze fruit thinly with a flat brush.
Serve Carousel des Fruits as a lunch, tea or dinner speciality.
The choux pastry ring may be frozen before assembly in a plastic bag for future use.
Freezing time 8 weeks.

JULY PANCAKES

1 lb/450 g soft summer fruits; strawberries, raspberries, peaches, kiwi fruit, bananas, black cherries.

PANCAKES:
4 eggs (size 3), separated

2 tablespoons clear honey

2 oz/50 g golden granulated sugar

2 oz/50 g whole meal flour

1 tablespoon cornflour

FILLING:
10 fl oz/300 ml natural yogurt

5 fl oz/150 ml double cream

1 tablespoon clear honey

TO DECORATE:
1 tablespoon icing sugar

serves 6–8
Preheat oven 425°F/220°C/gas mark 7

1. Put the yogurt into a coffee filter or muslin and leave to drain for 60 mins.
2. Line two baking sheets with greaseproof paper.
3. Separate the eggs into 2 mixing bowls.
4. Whisk the egg yolks with the clear honey to form a thick ribbon across the surface. Use an electric mixer for this procedure.
5. Whisk the egg whites with a clean whisk, gradually adding the sugar. Continue whisking until firm peaks are formed.. Carefully fold the beaten egg whites into yolks with a metal spoon.
6. Sieve the flour and cornflour together over the eggs and fold in with large metal spoon. Spoon the mixture onto the prepared trays, 3–4 per tray.
Spread each pancake into a 5 in/13 cm circle, and bake near the top of the oven for 10–12 mins.
7. Allow the pancakes to cool on the paper. They will keep in the refrigerator for several days or may be frozen for up to 8 weeks.
To complete the filling:
8. Loosely whip the cream with the honey, and blend with the now firm yogurt.
Put a spoonful of this cream onto each pancake, arrange the soft fruits over the cream and fold in half.

To finish:
Dust with icing sugar, and caramelize the sugar with a heated skewer.
July Pancakes will keep in the refrigerator for up to 48 hrs.

PÊCHES RAFRAÎCHIS BOURGUIGNONNE
Quite simply the best thing that could ever happen to peaches.

1 lb/450 g fresh raspberries

9 fl oz/250 ml good Beaujolais wine

2 tablespoons icing sugar

8 large peaches

2 oz/50 g flaked almonds (toasted)

serves 6

1. Reserve 18 raspberries for decoration. Purée the remaining fruit in a liquidizer, and rub through a fine sieve to remove the seeds. Add the Beaujolais and sweeten with a little icing sugar.
2. Throw the peaches into boiling water for 2–3 mins to loosen their skins.
3. Slice the peeled peaches into the sauce and chill for 3–4 hrs.
Serve in shallow glasses. Decorate with raspberries and toasted flaked almonds.
The peaches will keep in the sauce for up to 2 days or may be frozen for up to 3 weeks.

RASPBERRY TULIPS

Vanilla ice cream covered with a yogurt sauce, studded with fresh raspberries and captured within a delicate tulip biscuit.

TULIP BISCUIT:
2 oz/50 g soft butter

3 oz/85 g icing sugar

3 drops vanilla essence

2 egg whites (size 3)

3 oz/85 g plain flour

2 pt/1.1 litre Vanilla Ice Cream (see page 64)

1 lb/450 g fresh raspberries

5 fl oz/150 ml double cream

5 fl oz/150 ml natural yogurt

TO DECORATE:
spun sugar (see page 6)

serves 6
Preheat oven 400°F/205°C/gas mark 6

1. Grease two baking sheets and dust lightly with flour.
2. Weigh the ingredients for the tulip biscuits as accurately as possible to avoid disappointment.
Cream together the soft butter and icing sugar in a hand mixing bowl until pale in colour.
Add the vanilla essence and gradually beat in the egg whites.
3. Sieve in the flour and stir into a smooth paste.
To make the stencil:
4. Cut a 4 in/10 cm hole in a plastic ice cream carton and trim carton with a pair of scissors to within 1 in/2.5 cm of the hole.
Lay the stencil flat onto the baking sheet, and with a palette knife spread the biscuits onto their shapes, 3–4 per tray.
5. Bake the biscuits near the top of the oven for 10–12 mins.
As the biscuits come out of the oven, set them to cool in deep dishes. Have several dishes ready as the tulips will set very quickly.
Tulip biscuits will keep for up to a week when sealed in an airtight box.
To prepare the raspberry sauce:
6. Reserve 12 oz/350 g raspberries for decoration. Purée the remaining fruit and rub through a fine sieve.
7. Loosely whip the cream with a little icing sugar. Stir in the yogurt and add the raspberry purée.

To assemble:
8. Have ready the tulip biscuits, raspberry yogurt, vanilla ice cream and, if you choose, spun sugar.
Arrange each biscuit on a dessert plate, put a scooop of vanilla ice cream into each, pour over the sauce, stud with raspberries, and veil with spun sugar. Serve immediately.

PÊCHES CARDINAL

July peaches are enrobed in a sauce of fresh strawberries and yogurt, served with vanilla ice cream and Langues des Chats Biscuits.

6 ripe peaches

3 oz/85 g golden granulated sugar

8 oz/225 g English strawberries

5 fl oz/150 ml double cream

10 fl oz/300 ml natural yogurt

2 oz/50 g flaked almonds (toasted)

2 pt/1.1 litre Vanilla Ice Cream (see page 64)

serves 6

1. Blanch the peaches in boiling water to loosen their skins, or microwave for a short length of time. (Underripe fruits do not peel well.)
2. Prepare a light syrup from the sugar and 1 pt/600 ml water.
Simmer the peaches in the syrup for 10–12 mins, and leave to cool.
Reserve 6 good strawberries for decoration, and crush the remaining fruit in a plastic bag.
3. Loosely whip the cream with a little sugar if desired.
Blend the cream into the yogurt and fold in the crushed strawberries.
4. Drain the peaches onto a kitchen towel, remove the stones and arrange into individual coupe dishes.
Put a scoop of vanilla ice cream inside each peach, and cover with strawberry yogurt sauce.
Decorate with toasted flaked almonds and a whole strawberry.
Serve with Langues des Chats biscuits (see page 88).

Watermelon Fruit Basket

WATERMELON FRUIT BASKET

A most attractive way to serve fresh fruit salad at a buffet lunch or evening meal.

1 medium watermelon
1 tablespoon clear honey
2 tablespoons golden syrup
10 fl oz/300 ml orange juice
2 lb/900 g mixed summer fruits
3 fl oz/75 ml Maraschino or Kirsch
1 bunch fresh mint

serves 6–8

1. Place the watermelon on a chopping board with the stem facing away from you. Imagine the melon as a globe.
Cut a handle 1½ in/4 cm wide either side of the north pole down as far as the Equator. Cut a line at right angles from the handle along the Equator.
Try marking out the lines with felt pen as a guide.
Remove the two sections either side of the handle and loosen the flesh with a grapefruit knife.
2. Stir the honey and syrup into the orange juice.
3. Cut up the fruits into even-sized pieces and chill for several hours in the orange juice syrup.
To serve:
4. Stand the basket on crushed ice, fill with the prepared fruits and sprinkle with Maraschino or Kirsch.

AUGUST

Mango and Raspberry Mousseline; Fresh Figs à la Royale;
Wine and Yogurt Grape Torte; Pêches Nelly Melba;
Tarte aux Fruits Panaché; Blueberry Pancakes American Style;
Polka Dot Clouds; Roulade of Summer Fruits; Eton Mess;
Fresh Fig and Mēlon Cocktail with Raspberries;
Melon and Ginger Sorbet.

MANGO AND RASPBERRY MOUSSELINE

1 large ripe mango
12 oz/350 g fresh raspberries
2 teaspoons powdered gelatine
5 fl oz/150 ml double cream
5 fl oz/150 ml natural yogurt
2 egg whites
2 tablespoons golden granulated sugar
TO DECORATE: *5 fl oz/150 ml whipping fresh cream*
fresh mint

serves 6

1. Peel the mango with a sharp knife. Cut the flesh away from the flat stone. Reserve half of the flesh for decoration.
Liquidize the remaining mango, and rub through a fine sieve.
2. Reserve 6 oz/175 g of the best raspberries for decoration, purée the remaining fruit and pass through a fine sieve.
3. Put 3–4 raspberries in the bottom of 6 stem glasses. Cover with a tablespoon of mango purée, and leave to one side.
4. Soften the powdered gelatine in 2 tablespoons cold water, 2–3 mins.
Melt the gelatine over a saucepan of boiling water, and stir into raspberry purée.
5. Loosely whip the cream, and blend in the yogurt.
6. Whisk the egg whites with the sugar to form soft peaks.
7. Stir the setting raspberry purée into the cream and fold in the beaten egg whites. Pour the mousse into the prepared glasses and leave to set in the refrigerator for 1½–2 hrs.

To decorate:
8. Cut the reserved mango into thin slices, and arrange 3 slices on each mousse. Moisten with mango purée, and put a few raspberries to one side. Pipe on a small rosette of cream and finish with a fresh mint leaf.
Will keep in the refrigerator for up to 3 days.

FRESH FIGS À LA ROYALE
Moist little figs bound in a raspberry yogurt sauce, laced with brandy and chocolate liqueur. A touch of elegance fit for royalty.

8 ripe figs
11 oz/325 g fresh raspberries
SAUCE: *5 fl oz/150 ml natural yogurt*
5 fl oz/150 ml double cream
1 tablespoon icing sugar
4 tablespoons brandy
2 tablespoons chocolate liqueur
2 oz/50 g grated dark chocolate

serves 4

1. Put the yogurt into a coffee filter or muslin, and leave for 60 mins to drain.
2. Reserve 20 raspberries for decoration. Purée the remaining fruit, and rub through a fine sieve to remove the pips.
3. Loosely whip the cream with the icing sugar and blend in the strained yogurt. Stir in the raspberry purée, and flavour with brandy and chocolate liqueur.
4. Peel the figs with a sharp knife and arrange them in a shallow serving dish. Spoon the sauce over each fig and decorate with raspberries and grated chocolate.

WINE AND YOGURT GRAPE TORTE

Open your eyes to this featherlight creation. Well defined Muscat grapes are set within a mousseline of yogurt and white wine.

BISCUIT BASE:

4 oz/115 g digestive biscuits

2 oz/50 g unsalted butter

MOUSSE:

1 lb/450 g Muscat grapes

0.4 oz/11 g powdered gelatine

5 fl oz/150 ml double cream

5 fl oz/150 ml natural yogurt

3 fl oz/75 ml dry white wine

2 egg whites

2 tablespoons golden granulated sugar

TO DECORATE:

2 oz/50 g sponge crumbs

3 oz/85 g apricot preserve

serves 6

1. Line an 8 in/20 cm spring form cake tin with greaseproof paper.
2. Crush the digestive biscuits in a plastic bag, melt the butter in a saucepan, and stir in the crumbs.
3. Press the crumbs into the bottom of the cake tin, and leave to firm in the refrigerator.
4. Peel 4 oz/100 g grapes, and remove the pips with a clean hair grip.
Cut the remaining grapes in half, remove the pips, and leave to one side.
5. Soften the powdered gelatine in 4 tablespoons of cold water, 2–3 mins, and melt the gelatine over a saucepan of hot water.
6. Loosely whip the cream, and blend in the yogurt.
7. Add the wine to the melted gelatine, and stir into the yogurt cream.
8. Whisk the egg whites with the sugar until they form soft peaks (see page 00).Carefully fold into the now setting mousse.
9. Add the peeled grapes, and pour into the prepared tin.
Leave to set for at least 2 hrs in the refrigerator.
If you wish, the gâteau may be frozen at this stage for later use, 6–8 weeks.

To decorate:
10. Release the gâteau from the tin and remove the greaseproof paper. Mask the sides with sponge crumbs, and decorate the top with grape halves.
To finish:
11. Dilute the apricot preserve with 1 tablespoon of water, bring to boil and glaze thinly with a flat brush.
Wine and Yogurt Grape Torte will keep in the refrigerator for up to 3 days.

PÊCHES NELLY MELBA

This well known dessert was invented by Auguste Escoffier in 1893, then at the Ritz Hotel London. Dame Nelly Melba had arrived late one evening with her guests to a largely empty restaurant. Aiming to please, Escoffier prepared for her what he could from what was left. Dame Nelly was to enjoy her newly created peach confection named after her beautiful self.

6 large peaches

4 oz/115 g golden granulated sugar

1 lb/450 g fresh raspberries

2 pt/1.1 litre Vanilla Ice Cream (see page 64)

5 fl oz/150 ml double cream

1 tablespoon icing sugar

serves 6

1. Throw the peaches into a saucepan of boiling water to loosen their skins, or microwave briefly.
2. Prepare a light syrup from the sugar and 2pts/1 litre water. Poach the peaches in the syrup for 10–15 mins.
3. Reserve 18 perfect raspberries for decoration.
Purée the remaining fruit, rub through a fine sieve, and sweeten with a little icing sugar.
To serve:
4. Choose 6 large dessert plates. Slice the peaches and arrange on the plates in a fan shape. Prepare this before the main course.
5. Arrange two balls of vanilla ice cream to one side, and pour the raspberry sauce into the remaining space. Decorate with whole raspberries, flaked almonds and a rosette of fresh cream.
Serve with Autumn Leaf Biscuits (see page 89).

TARTE AUX FRUITS PANACHÉ
A symphony of seasonal colour seated on fine yogurt filling.

1 × recipe Whole Meal Biscuit Pastry (see page 91)

1½ lb/675 g mixed summer fruits: raspberries, strawberries, peaches, bananas, kiwi fruit, grapes

FILLING:
2 egg yolks

5 fl oz/150 ml natural yogurt

1 tablespoon golden granulated sugar

2 level tablespoons cornflour

fresh vanilla pod

5 fl oz/150 ml milk

TO GLAZE:
3 oz/85 g redcurrant jelly

serves 6 .
Preheat oven 400°F/205°C/gas mark 6

1. Lightly grease a 9 in/23 cm flan ring, and line with biscuit pastry.
Rest the flan for 20 mins, and bake blind, 25–30 mins.
To prepare the yogurt filling:
2. Separate the egg yolks into a basin, add the yogurt, and stir in the sugar.
3. Dilute the cornflour with 4 tablespoons cold water, and stir into the yogurt.
4. Split the vanilla pod down the middle to release the tiny black seeds. Bring the milk to boil with the vanilla pod, and pour over the yogurt. Return to the saucepan, and stir back to boil to thicken. Turn the yogurt cream into a clean basin and leave to cool.
5. Cut the chosen fruits into even sized pieces, as for fruit salad. Toss the fruits in a large bowl as evenly as possible.
6. Spread an even layer of the yogurt cream into the bottom of the pre-baked flan case, and pile in the mixed fruits.
To finish:
7. Melt the redcurrant jelly over a slow heat, and glaze flan thinly with a flat brush.
Tarte aux Fruits Panaché is best enjoyed the day made, although the filling and flan may be frozen separately for up to 6 weeks.

BLUEBERRY PANCAKES AMERICAN STYLE
American-style pancakes are quick and easy to make. Americans enjoy them for breakfast with butter and maple syrup, on the Continent they are favoured at the end of a meal with vanilla ice cream.

4 oz/115 g whole meal flour

2 oz/50 g self raising flour

2 tablespoons granulated sugar

1 oz/25 g salted butter

8 fl oz/250 ml milk

1 egg (size 3)

3 oz/85 g blueberries

2 pts/1.1 litre Vanilla Ice Cream (see page 64)

serves 6

1. Sieve the two flours together into a mixing bowl, and add the sugar.
2. Brown the butter in a large nonstick frying-pan.
Pour the nut brown butter into the milk and beat in the egg.
3. Make a well in the centre of the flour, add all the liquid and stir into a thick batter.
4. Lastly add the blueberries. (Sultanas soaked in dark rum are an interesting alternative)
5. Heat the frying-pan over a steady heat; nonstick pans do not need additional fat.
6. Spoon the batter into small heaps, and let them spread to a diameter of 3 in/7.5 cm. As soon as bubbles break on the surface turn them over and cook for a further 30 secs. Keep the pancakes under a tea towel until ready to serve.
The pancakes can be made several hours before your guests arrive and warmed in a conventional oven or microwave.
7. Serve the pancakes with a generous scoop of Vanilla Ice Cream.
American Style Pancakes freeze successfully between pieces of greaseproof paper, 6–8 weeks.

POLKA DOT CLOUDS

1 pt/575 ml milk

½ fresh vanilla pod

4 eggs separated

2 oz/50 g golden granulated sugar

6 oz/170 g redcurrants

CUSTARD SAUCE:
1 tablespoon custard powder

2 tablespoons milk

4 egg yolks

1 tablespoon golden granulated sugar

TO DECORATE:
pink spun sugar (see page 6)

serves 6

1. Pour the milk into a large skillet, add the vanilla pod and simmer gently.
2. Separate the egg whites into a clean mixing bowl, add the sugar and whisk until firm. Strip the redcurrants from their stalks, and fold them into the soft meringue.

3. Shape the meringue between two tablespoons, dipped in hot water, and poach in the milk, turning once, 2–3 mins. Retain the milk for the custard.
4. Cover a tray with a damp tea-towel, and lay the meringue shapes in rows. Poached meringue will keep for up to 8 hrs in a refrigerator.
To prepare the sauce:
5. Dilute the custard powder with 2 tablespoons cold milk, stir in the egg yolks, and add the sugar.
6. Transfer the poaching milk into a saucepan, bring to boil, and pour over the custard mixture. Return to a slow heat and stir to a gentle boil until thickened slightly. Remove the vanilla pod, and leave to cool.
To serve:
7. Pour the custard sauce into a glass bowl, and arrange the clouds of meringue over the top.
Chill and serve with a veil of pink spun sugar.

ROULADE OF SUMMER FRUITS

A delicious assortment of soft fruits rolled up in a carpet sponge with a smooth yogurt cream.

Roulade of Summer Fruits

1 × recipe Blanket Swiss Roll (see page 93)

5 fl oz/150 ml double cream

1 tablespoon icing sugar

5 fl oz/150 ml natural yogurt

1 lb/450 g soft summer fruits; raspberries, peaches, strawberries, kiwi fruit.

TO DECORATE:
5 fl oz/150 ml double cream

4 oz/115 g soft fruits

serves 4–6

To assemble:
1. Loosely whip the cream with icing sugar, and blend in the yogurt.
2. Spread a thin layer over the sponge, scatter over the soft fruits and roll up tightly.
3. Decorate with rosettes of whipped cream, and pieces of soft fruit.
Chill well before serving.
The Roulade may be frozen for up to 6 weeks before final decoration.

ETON MESS

Some desserts are literally thrown together. This is one of them.

8 oz/225 g fresh raspberries
8 oz/225 g blackberries
10 fl oz/300 ml double cream
1 tablespoon icing sugar
7 oz/200 g low fat soft cheese
squeeze of lemon

serves 8

1. Reserve 8 raspberries, and 8 blackberries for decoration.
Put the remaining fruits in a bowl and crush with a wooden spoon.
2. Loosely whip the cream with a little icing sugar to sweeten.
Blend in the soft cheese, add a squeeze of lemon, and stir in the crushed raspberries and blackberries.
3. Divide the mixture between 8 stem glasses, and decorate with the reserved fruits.
Eton Mess will keep in the refrigerator for up to 48 hrs before serving.

FRESH FIG AND MELON COCKTAIL WITH RASPBERRIES

Perfumed Charantais melon, the first of the year's figs, and the sweetest of summer raspberries, present themselves in a fine yogurt sauce.

2 Charantais melons
5 fl oz/150 ml natural yogurt
1 tablespoon stem ginger syrup
2 dark figs
8 oz/225 g fresh raspberries

serves 4

1. Cut the melons in half, discard the seeds, and scoop out as many melon balls as you can with a melon baller.
2. Liquidize the remaining flesh, and rub through a fine sieve.
Measure 3 fl oz/75 ml of the purée into the yogurt, and add ginger syrup to sweeten.
Keep this sauce in the refrigerator until needed.
3. To prepare the figs; wash them carefully and cut away the stem. If the skins are soft and tender, they may be eaten, otherwise peel them with a sharp knife.
To serve the cocktail:
4. Pour off any juices from the melon balls, and fold into the yogurt sauce.
5. Cut the figs in half from top to bottom, slice the fruit into thin wedges, and arrange on a large dessert plate. Position the melon balls to one side, and sprinkle with fresh raspberries.
If you have room in your refrigerator, it is a good idea to prepare this dessert some time before the meal.

GINGER AND MELON SORBET

A most attractive way to serve Cantaloup melons, blended with mild ginger and honey, frozen and put back into their skins. Ginger and Melon Sorbet may be served as a starter or dessert.

2 Cantaloup melons
1 oz/25 g stem ginger
2 tablespoons ginger syrup
2 tablespoons clear honey
6 sprigs fresh mint

serves 6

1. Cut melons in half from top to bottom, remove the seeds and cut each half into 4. Scoop out the flesh from each section, and freeze the skins for later use.
2. Liquidize the flesh with the stem ginger, ginger syrup, and honey to make a fine purée.
Freeze the purée in a metal bowl for 60 mins.
Whisk the sorbet to break up any pieces of ice, return to the freezer, and whisk every 20 mins until quite firm. A further $1\frac{1}{2}$ hrs.
3. To fill the melon skins; lay each melon skin on its side on a piece of greaseproof paper, spread in the sorbet level with the cut edge and return the slices to the freezer, still on their sides, until needed.
To serve:
4. Leave the melon slices in the refrigerator to soften while the main course is served, 20–25 mins.
5. Arrange two slices per person on a dessert plate, and decorate with a sprig of fresh mint.
Offer Savoy Biscuits as an accompaniment

SEPTEMBER

*Charlotte of Kiwi Fruit and Pernod; Apricot and Greengage Flan;
Blackcurrant and Yogurt Mousseline; English Plums in Red Wine;
Apple Flower Flan; Spiced Ginger Pears; Fresh Fig and Raspberry
Cheese;
Continental Plum Flan; Wine Jelly Cocktails; Poires Dijonnaise;
Tarte aux Pommes Chaud; Vanilla Ice Cream; Blackberry and Pear
Mousses.*

CHARLOTTE OF KIWI FRUIT AND PERNOD

*The unique flavour of aniseed was destined to accompany
these subtle little fruits of New Zealand.*

SPONGE:

3 eggs (size 3)

3 oz/85 g golden granulated sugar

2 oz/50 g whole meal flour

1 oz/25 g plain cake flour

MOUSSE:

5 fl oz/150 ml natural yogurt

5 fl oz/150 ml double cream

0.4 oz/11 g powdered gelatine

2 eggs (size 3)

2 oz/50 g golden granulated sugar

2 fl oz/50 ml Pernod or Marie Brizzard Anisette

TO DECORATE:

4 kiwi fruit

2oz/50 g apricot preserve

5 fl oz/150 ml whipped cream

4 oz/115 g fresh strawberries

serves 8
Preheat oven 425°F/220°C/gas mark 7

To prepare the sponge:
1. Line a large baking sheet with greaseproof paper.
2. Sieve the flour onto another piece of paper and put to one side.
3. Separate the eggs into 2 clean mixing bowls.
Whisk the egg yolks with half of the sugar until the whisk will leave a trail across the surface. Use your machine mixer for this.
Whisk the egg whites with the remaining sugar until they form stiff peaks.
4. Fold the beaten egg whites into yolks with a large metal spoon. Gradually fold in the flour until quite smooth.

5. Put the sponge mixture into a piping bag fitted with a $\frac{1}{4}$ in/6 mm plain nozzle and pipe the mixture into long lines that just touch each other.
6. Bake the sponge in the top of the oven for 10–12 mins. This particular sponge will freeze for up to 3 months.
To prepare the mould:
7. Choose an 8 in/20 cm loose-bottomed cake tin and line with greaseproof paper. Cut the sponge across the ridges to the depth of the cake tin.
Cut the remaining pieces to fit into the bottom of the tin.
To prepare the mousse:
8. Soften the gelatine in 4 tablespoons cold water, 2–3 mins, and melt by standing in a saucepan of hot water.
9. Loosely whip the cream with half of the sugar. Stir in the yogurt and add Pernod to taste.
10. Separate the egg yolks into the cream. Put the whites in a clean bowl, add the remaining sugar and whisk the egg whites until they form soft peaks.
11. Stir the melted gelatine into yogurt cream, fold in the soft meringue, pour into the prepared mould and leave to set for at least 2 hrs in the refrigerator.
To decorate:
12. Remove the fine skins from the kiwi fruit with a sharp knife.
Slice the fruits thinly and arrange on the mousse.
13. Dilute the apricot preserve with 1 tablespoon water, bring to boil and glaze thinly with a flat brush.
Decorate with rosettes of whipped cream and strawberries.
The Charlotte will keep in the refrigerator for up to 3 days. Or it may be frozen before decoration for 8 weeks.
Almost any soft fruit can be displayed on the Charlotte. Substitute the Pernod for Kirsch, and decorate with peaches, raspberries, strawberries, mangoes, blackberries, cherries, or a mixture of tropical fruits.

APRICOT AND GREENGAGE FLAN

1 × recipe Whole Meal Biscuit Pastry (see page 91)

6 oz/170 g dried apricots

1½ lb/675 g greengages

TO DECORATE:
3 oz/85 g apricot preserve

1 oz/25 g pistachio nuts or almonds

serves 5–6
Preheat oven 375°F/190°C/gas mark 5

1. Lightly grease a 9 in/23 cm flan ring and line with biscuit pastry.
2. Roughly chop the apricots, and spread them into the bottom of the flan case.
3. Halve the greengages, and remove the stones. Arrange in a flower pattern starting at the outside edge of the flan, and working to the centre.
4. Bake the flan in centre oven for 50 mins.
To finish:
5. Dilute the apricot preserve with 1 tablespoon water, bring to boil and glaze flan thinly with a flat brush.
Decorate with halves of pistachio nut or almond and serve warm or cold with vanilla ice cream.
Apricot and Greengage Flan will keep in an airtight tin for up to 3 days. It does not freeze well.

BLACKCURRANT AND YOGURT MOUSSELINE

4 oz/115 g blackcurrants

0.4 oz/11 g powdered gelatine

5 fl oz/150 ml double cream

10 fl oz/300 ml natural yogurt

2 egg whites

2 oz/50 g golden granulated sugar

TOPPING:
6 oz/170 g blackcurrants

2 tablespoons golden granulated sugar

4 fl oz/100 ml water

1 level teaspoon cornflour

serves 6

1. Purée of ripe blackcurrants in a liquidizer, and rub through a fine sieve.
2. Moisten the gelatine with 2 tablespoons cold water, and melt over a saucepan of hot water.
Add the melted gelatine to the blackcurrant purée, and leave to one side.
3. Loosely whip the cream, blend in the yogurt, and stir in the blackcurrant purée.
4. Whisk the egg whites with the sugar until they form soft peaks. Carefully fold the soft meringue into the now setting mousseline. Pour the mixture into 6 stem glasses, and leave in the refrigerator to set 1½–2 hrs.
To prepare the topping:
5. Make a light syrup from the sugar and water in a stainless saucepan. Simmer the remaining blackcurrants for 2–3 mins in the syrup.
6. Dilute the cornflour in 2 tablespoons of cold water, and use to thicken the blackcurrant syrup.
To finish:
7. Spread the cooled topping over the set mousseline, and decorate with a few blackcurrant leaves.
Blackcurrant and Yogurt Mousseline will keep in the refrigerator for 3 days.

ENGLISH PLUMS IN RED WINE

A bottle of house red rarely goes unnoticed in a pot of poaching plums. Serve them with lashings of fresh cream or yogurt.

5 oz/140 g golden granulated sugar

1 pt/575 ml water

15 fl oz/450 ml red wine

1 cinnamon stick

2 lb/900 g ripe plums

serves 6
Preparation 10 mins.

1. Prepare a light syrup from the sugar and water, add the wine, and simmer gently with the cinnamon stick for 8–10 mins.
2. Wash the plums and remove any stalks. Poach the fruit in the syrup for not longer than 10 mins. Overcooking will spoil their shape and goodness.
Allow the plums to rest in their syrup until quite cold. Poached plums will keep in the refrigerator for up to 4 days or they may be frozen successfully for up to 3 months.
Serve the plums in a glass or porcelain bowl.

Apple Flower Flan

APPLE FLOWER FLAN

1 × recipe Hazelnut and Cinnamon Pastry (see page 92)

1 ½ lb/675 g English dessert apples

FILLING:
10 fl oz/300 ml cold milk

½ teaspoon vanilla essence

2 egg yolks

2 tablespoons soft brown sugar

5 level tablespoons plain flour

½ teaspoon ground cinnamon

TO FINISH:
3oz/85 g apricot preserve

serves 6
Preheat oven 375°F/190°C/gas mark 5

1. Lightly grease an 8 in/23 cm flan ring, and line with pastry.
To prepare the filling:
2. Separate the yolks into a basin, add 2 tablespoons of the cold milk, and whisk in the flour and sugar.

3. Bring the remaining milk to boil with the vanilla, and pour over the beaten yolks. Return the mixture to the saucepan over a gentle heat. Stir the custard to simmer until quite thick.
Add ground cinnamon.
4. Spread a ¾ in/2 cm layer of custard filling into the unbaked flan case.
5. Peel and quarter apples, and slice them thinly on a vegetable slicer.
Starting at the edge of the flan, arrange the slices so that they overlap closely in a clockwise direction. When you have reached the point at which you started, begin to spiral towards the centre.
When the flower pattern is complete, sprinkle with fine sugar and bake in centre oven for 45–50 mins.
To glaze the flan:
6. Dilute apricot preserve with 1 tablespoon of water, bring to the boil and glaze flan thinly with a flat brush. Decorate with half a green grape in the centre.
Serve Apple Flower Flan warm or cold with a thin custard sauce or pouring cream.
Best eaten on the day of making.

SPICED GINGER PEARS

3 tablespoons honey
4 tablespoons ginger syrup
2 pts/1.1 litre water
1 orange
1 cinnamon stick
2 whole cloves
3 oz/85 g stem ginger
2 oz/50 g sultanas
6 small pears
2 tablespoons cornflour
2 pts/1.1 litre Chocolate Ice Cream

serves 6

1. Prepare a light syrup from the honey, ginger syrup and water.
2. Remove the zest from the orange with a vegetable peeler, and cut into thin strips. Add to the syrup with the cinnamon stick, cloves, stem ginger and sultanas.
3. Peel the pears whole, and remove their insides from the underside with a melon baller.
Poach in the prepared syrup for 25–30 mins.
4. Remove the pears from the syrup. Dilute the cornflour with 4 tablespoons of cold water. Stir into the boiling syrup, and allow to thicken to the consistency of single cream.
5. Return the pears to the syrup, and leave to cool.
Spiced Ginger Pears are served with chocolate ice cream, and if desired a little pouring cream.
The pears will keep in the refrigerator for several days, or will freeze for up to 6 weeks.

FRESH FIG AND RASPBERRY CHEESE

1 lb/450 g fresh raspberries
7 oz/200 g low fat soft cheese or quark
5 fl oz/150 ml natural yogurt
1 tablespoon icing sugar
1 tablespoon lemon juice
12 ripe figs

serves 6

1. Purée 5 oz/150 g raspberries, and rub them through a fine sieve.
Put 3 tablespoons of this purée to one side for decoration.
2. Blend together the soft cheese and yogurt (30 secs in food processor).
Add the raspberry purée, icing sugar, and lemon juice.
3. Wash and dry the figs, remove the stem, and cut each fruit into 4, but leaving the fruit intact.
Arrange the figs, 2 per person on a large plate. Open each fig out slightly, and put a good spoonful of the raspberry cheese into the centre of each.
Decorate with a neat pile of raspberries to one side, and a swirl of raspberry purée in the abounding sauce. Chill well before serving.

CONTINENTAL PLUM FLAN

1 × recipe Whole Meal Biscuit Pastry (see page 91)
2 tablespoons bran fibre
1½ lb/675 g sweet Victoria plums
1 egg (size 3)
3 fl oz/75 ml double cream
1 teaspoon clear honey

TO GLAZE:
3 oz/85 g apricot preserve

serves 6
Preheat oven 375°F/190°C/gas mark 5

1. Lightly grease a 9 in/23 cm flan tin, and line with biscuit pastry.
Sprinkle bran fibre into the bottom of the flan. (This will absorb any juices expelled during cooking.)
2. Cut the plums into 4 and arrange the fruit standing up like a flower. If the plums are a little tart, sprinkle on a little sugar to taste.
3. Bake the flan in centre oven for 45–50 mins.
4. Beat the egg into the cream, stir in the honey and strain over the plums.
Return the flan to the oven for 10–12 mins until the custard has set lightly.
To glaze the flan:
5. Dilute the apricot preserve with 1 tablespoon of water, bring to boil and glaze flan thinly with a flat brush.
Serve Continental Plum Flan warm or cold with a ball of vanilla ice cream. The flan is best eaten the day made.

WINE JELLY COCKTAILS

18 fl oz/550 ml dry white wine
3 oz/85 g golden granulated sugar
1 lemon
0.4 oz/11 g powdered gelatine
8 oz/225 g Muscat grapes
2 ripe peaches
8 oz/225 g strawberries
TO DECORATE: 5 fl oz/150 ml whipped cream

serves 6

1. Prepare a light syrup from the sugar, wine and lemon juice.
2. Soften the powdered gelatine in 4 tablespoons cold water, 2–3 mins.
3. Remove the wine syrup from the heat, and stir in the gelatine.
4. Peel and de-seed the grapes, dice the peaches and arrange in 6 stem glasses.
Pour in a little jelly, and leave to set, 20 mins.
Select 6 strawberries for decoration. Slice the rest and arrange on top of the dishes.
5. Add the final layer of jelly, and leave to set once more.
Decorate each jelly with a small rosette of whipped cream and a strawberry. Note the jelly should be only just set, few people enjoy rubber jellies.
A variation of this recipe could make use of Port, strawberries and a dash of Grand Marnier.

POIRES DIJONNAISE

Dijon is well known for its crop of blackcurrants. The locals are particularly fond of this simple combination of pears and blackcurrants, said to put colour in their cheeks.

6 oz/170 g golden granulated sugar
2pt/1.1 litre water
1 lemon
6 small pears
1 lb/450 g fresh blackcurrants
2 tablespoons cornflour

serves 6

1. Prepare a light syrup from the sugar and water, add the zest of lemon, and squeeze in the juice.
2. Peel the pears, leaving the stalks on, remove the inside of each pear from the underside with a melon baller.
Poach the pears in the syrup for 25–30 mins depending upon their ripeness.
3. Remove the blackcurrants from their stalks, and poach them with the pears for a further 3–4 mins.
4. Dilute the cornflour with 3 tablespoons cold water, and use to thicken the cooking liquid.
5. Chill the pears in their juices for several hours before serving in a glass or china bowl. The flavour of the pears will improve considerably if they are kept for several days in the refrigerator.
Serve with sour cream or yogurt.

TARTE AUX POMMES CHAUD

When your eyes have deceived your appetite, try this French Swiss speciality of caramelized apples on a carpet ride of flaky pastry.

3 oz/75 g short crust or puff pastry trimmings
2 English dessert apples
1 tablespoon fine sugar – caster or icing sugar
1 oz/25 g butter

serves 2–3
Preheat oven 450°F/230°C/gas mark 8

1. Roll out the pastry as thinly as possible, and cut out a large circle, 9 in/23 cm the size of a dinner plate.
Leave the pastry to rest for at least 30 mins on a baking sheet.
If you have time, other bases can be made for the freezer for later use (6–8 weeks).
Freeze between pieces of greaseproof paper.
2. Peel, core and slice the apples as thinly as possible. Arrange the apples over the pastry base completely covering the surface.
Sprinkle with sugar, and dot with pieces of butter.
3. Bake the tart in a fierce oven for 10–15 mins, allowing the apples to colour well.
Serve Tarte aux Pommes Chaud straight from the oven with vanilla ice cream or cream.

VANILLA ICE CREAM

Few people have experienced real vanilla ice cream. I can assure you the taste of fresh vanilla is quite unforgettable. Great care is needed during the preparation of the egg custard, the resulting ice cream is well worth the effort.

4 egg yolks

2 oz/50 g vanilla sugar

8 fl oz/250 ml milk

5 fl oz/150 ml double cream

½ fresh vanilla pod (split)

serves 4–5

Before you begin, please read the method carefully.
1. Separate the egg yolks into a basin, and stir in the vanilla sugar.
2. Bring the milk and cream to boil with the split vanilla pod.
Pour the boiling milk over the egg yolks and sugar, and stir.
Return the custard to the saucepan.
At this stage the custard must on no account boil, unless scrambled eggs are on the menu.
3. Stir the custard over the lowest heat possible, using a flat bottomed wooden spoon. When the custard has thickened to the consistency of single cream, 1–2 mins, transfer immediately to a clean basin. This will arrest the cooking; curdling is now out of the question.
Pour the egg custard through a fine sieve, and leave to cool.
The best results are obtained in an ice cream maker, although an acceptable ice cream can be made in a standard freezer.
Freeze the custard in a metal bowl, preferably stainless steel, for 60 mins. Whisk the ice cream every 20 mins until firm, a further 1½ hrs.
Vanilla Ice Cream is at its best when freshly made, although it will keep in the freezer for up to 3 weeks. Allow the ice cream to stand in the refrigerator for at last 20 mins before serving as hard ice cream is almost impossible to serve.
To make Coffee Ice Cream: add 1 tablespoon instant coffee to the boiling milk before adding the eggs.
For Chocolate Ice Cream; melt in 4 oz/115 g dark chocolate.

BLACKBERRY AND PEAR MOUSSES

2 oz/50 g golden granulated sugar

4 fl oz/100 ml water

1 cinnamon stick

1 lemon (zest)

1 lb/450 g new season pears

6 oz/170 g blackberries

2 teaspoons powdered gelatine

5 fl oz/150 ml double cream

5 fl oz/150 ml natural yogurt

2 egg whites

2 tablespoons golden granulated sugar

TO DECORATE:
8 oz/225 g blackberries

1 poached pear

serves 6

1. Prepare a light syrup from the sugar and water. Add the cinnamon stick and a large piece of lemon zest. Use a vegetable peeler to remove the zest cleanly.
2. Peel, core and slice the pears thinly. Cook in the syrup until soft, 15–20 mins.
Remove the lemon zest and save for decoration.
3. Add the blackberries to the syrup and liquidize the whole in a food processor. Rub the resulting purée through a fine sieve to remove any nasty pips and things.
4. Soften the powdered gelatine in 2 tablespoons cold water, 2–3 mins.
Then dissolve into the warm purée, and allow to cool.
5. Loosely whip the cream, and blend in the yogurt.
Fold into the setting fruit purée with a metal spoon.
6. Whisk the egg whites with the sugar until they form a soft peak.
7. Fold the soft egg whites into the fruit cream, retaining as much air as possible.
Pour the mousse into 6 decorative glasses, and leave to set for 1½–2 hrs.
To decorate:
8. Cover each mousse with slices of poached pear, blackberries, and a twist of lemon zest. The mousses will keep in the refrigerator for up to 3 days before decoration.

Blackberry and Pear Mousse

OCTOBER

*Walnut and Butterscotch Flan; Poires vin Rouge au Cannelle;
Apple and Hazelnut Flan; Poires Belle Hélène;
Chestnut Vermicelli; Taunton Turnovers; Pumpkin Soufflé;
Butter Pecan Pie; Apple and Cinnamon Custards;
Little Chocolate Pots.*

WALNUT AND BUTTERSCOTCH FLAN

*Without doubt the Swiss are a nation of nut lovers. This is
one of their favourites to mark the new season of walnuts.*

1 × recipe Whole Meal Biscuit Pastry (see page 91)

FILLING:

4 oz/115 g golden granulated sugar

2 tablespoons clear honey

6 tablespoons double cream

2 oz/50 g butter

6 oz/170 g walnut halves

serves 6
Preheat oven 375°F/190°C/gas mark 5

1. Lightly grease a 9 in/23 cm flan ring, and line with biscuit pastry. Allow to rest for 20 mins.
2. Put the sugar and honey into a heavy-bottomed saucepan and dissolve over a low heat. Boil rapidly for 5 mins until lightly caramelized.
Remove the pan from the heat, and add the butter and cream. Allow to cool slightly, then add the walnuts.
3. Turn the walnuts and sauce into the uncooked flan case. Don't worry if the mixture is still warm.
4. Bake the flan in oven for 35–40 mins. Allow the flan to cool completely before serving as a lunch or teatime dessert.
Walnut and Butterscotch Flan will keep for up to 10 days in an airtight biscuit tin. It does not freeze well.

POIRES VIN ROUGE AU CANNELLE

*Little pears poached in red wine and spices are a great
favourite at dinner parties. They are easy to prepare and keep
well in their natural juices.*

1 × 750 ml bottle red wine

10 fl oz/300 ml water

6 oz/170 g golden granulated sugar

1 cinnamon stick

1 bay leaf

4 whole allspice

12 small pears

2 level tablespoons cornflour

serves 6

1. Prepare a syrup from the red wine, water and sugar.
Add the spices and simmer gently for 10 mins.
2. Peel the pears whole, and remove their insides from the underside with a melon baller.
Poach in the syrup for 25–30 mins.
3. Remove the fruit from the syrup, dilute the cornflour with 4 tablespoons cold water, return to boil, and thicken to the consistency of single cream.
Return the pears to the syrup, and serve them warm or cold with natural yogurt or cream.
The pears will keep for up to 4 days in the refrigerator, or may be frozen for up to 6 weeks.

APPLE AND HAZELNUT FLAN

*Not just any old apple flan. Apples, hazelnuts and cinnamon
rendezvous within the boundaries of a light biscuity pastry.*

1 × recipe Hazelnut and Cinnamon Pastry (see
   page 92)

2 lb/900 g English dessert apples

½ lemon

1 teaspoon ground cinnamon

pinch ground cloves

1 tablespoon soft brown sugar

1 oz/25 g butter

TO GLAZE:
3 oz/85 g apricot preserve

serves 6
Preheat oven 400°F/205°C/gas mark 6.

1. Lightly grease a 9 in/23 cm flan ring and
line with hazelnut pastry. Rest the flan in the
refrigerator for 30 mins.
2. Peel and core all but 3 of the apples. Cut
the apples up finely, and put them in a
saucepan with the juice of ½ lemon,
cinnamon and clove. Cover with a lid and
simmer gently for 10–12 mins.
If the purée is still moist allow the steam to
escape by removing the lid. Adjust the
sweetness with 1 tablespoon sugar.
3. Allow the apples to cool slightly, and
spread on the bottom of the uncooked flan.
4. Wash the remaining apples and remove
cores.
Slice the apples thinly, and arrange over the
cooked apples to form an attractive design.
Dot the surface with pieces of butter, and
sprinkle with fine sugar.
5. Bake the flan in centre oven for 45 mins.
To finish the flan:
6. Dilute the apricot preserve with 1
tablespoon water, bring to the boil, and glaze
flan thinly with a flat brush.
Serve Apple and Hazelnut flan warm or cold
with vanilla ice cream or yogurt. Best
enjoyed the day made.

POIRES BELLE HÉLÈNE

*The perfect pear is poached in a light vanilla syrup, and
served with a hot chocolate sauce, vanilla ice cream, and a
sprinkling of toasted flaked almonds.*

6 oz/170 g golden granulated sugar

2 pts/1.1 litre water

1 lemon

1 cinnamon stick

1 fresh vanilla pod

6 dessert pears of an even size

CHOCOLATE SAUCE:
3 fl oz/75 ml milk

5 fl oz/150 ml double cream

1 tablespoon clear honey

7 oz/200 g bitter chocolate

TO DECORATE:
3 fl oz/75 g whipped cream

2 pt/1.1 litre Vanilla Ice cream (see page 64)

2 oz/50 g toasted flaked almonds

serves 6

1. Prepare a light syrup from the sugar and
water. Add the zest and juice of the lemon,
cinnamon, and the vanilla pod.
2. Peel the pears whole and remove their
insides from the underside with a melon
baller.
3. Poach the fruit in the prepared syrup for
25–30 mins, depending on their ripeness.
The flavour of the fruit will improve
considerably if the pears are left to stand in
their juices for a day or so.
To prepare the chocolate sauce:
4. Bring the milk and the cream to boil with
the honey.
Add the chocolate in small pieces, and stir
until dissolved. Keep the sauce warm by
standing in a saucepan of hot water until
needed.
To serve:
5. Drain the pears and stand them up on a
large dessert plate. Pour on a thin layer of
hot chocolate sauce, spoon a thin ribbon of
loosely whipped cream through the sauce to
create a simple pattern. Lastly arrange two
scoops of vanilla ice cream to one side, and
sprinkle on a few roasted flaked almonds.
Serve with Autumn Leaf Biscuits (see page
89).

Vermicelli Chestnut

Butter Pecan Pie
Recipe on page 70

CHESTNUT VERMICELLI

1 large tin sweet chesnut purée

5 fl oz/150 ml single cream

2 fl oz/50 ml Kirsch or Armagnac

TO FINISH:
8 broken meringue pieces

5 fl oz/150 ml natural yogurt

5 fl oz/150 ml double cream

pieces of sweet chestnut and angelica

serves 8
Preheat oven 400°F/205°C/gas mark 6

1. Blend together the chesnut purée, Kirsch, and cream.
If necessary, sweeten with a little icing sugar.
2. Prepare the tulip biscuits.
3. Loosely whip the cream with a little sugar if desired, and blend with the yogurt.
4. Put each tulip biscuit on a dessert plate, and arrange layers of yogurt cream and broken meringue.
Put the chestnut cream into a piping bag fitted with a vermicelli nozzle. Pipe the chestnut into a vermicelli over the broken meringue and decorate with a piece of chocolate and angelica.
Serve within 20 mins of assembly.

TAUNTON TURNOVERS

A delightful recollection of a town in Somerset. Taunton Turnovers are enjoyed at lunch or teatime with a dollop of west country cream.

8 oz/225 g Puff Pastry (see page 90)

1 lb/450 g Russet apples

2 fl oz/50 ml dry cider

1 tablespoon soft brown sugar

½ teaspoon ground cinnamon

pinch ground cloves

serves 8
Preheat oven 400°F/205°C/gas mark 6

1. Roll out the puff pastry into a rectangle 12 × 16 in/30 × 40 cm.
Cut out 16 × 4 in/10 cm squares and leave to rest for at least 35 mins.
To prepare the filling:
2. Peel, core and dice the apples. Throw them into a saucepan with the cider, sugar, and spices. Simmer uncovered for 5–6 mins. Taste the fruit for sweetness, and cool on a flat tray.
3. Put a teaspoon of cooked apple onto each square of pastry. Moisten the edges with beaten egg, and fold each in half from corner to corner. Moisten with water, dip the top side in fine sugar, and arrange on a lightly greased baking sheet. Bake the turnovers near the top of the oven for 25–30 mins.
Serve Taunton Turnovers warm or cold with a generous helping of West Country cream. The turnovers freeze well prior to baking, 8 weeks.

PUMPKIN SOUFFLÉ

If only for the sheer pleasure, Pumpkin Soufflé should be enjoyed with the closest of friends at the end of a perfect meal.

1 lb/450 g raw pumpkin
1 oz/25 g butter
½ teaspoon salt
2 teaspoons ground cinnamon
½ teaspoon ground ginger
pinch fresh nutmeg
CUSTARD BASE: *5 eggs (size 3), separated*
½ pt/300 ml milk
4 tablespoons plain flour
2 tablespoons golden granulated sugar
3 tablespoons golden granulated sugar

serves 4
Preheat oven 425°F/220°C/gas mark 7

1. Remove the seeds from the pumpkin, and cut the flesh away from the skin. Put the pumpkin into a large saucepan with butter, salt and the spices. Cover, and simmer for 10–12 mins.
Rub the resulting purée through a fine sieve or blend in a food processor for 60 secs.
To make the custard base:
2. Separate 5 egg yolks into a basin, add 2 tablespoons cold milk, and whisk in the flour and sugar.
Bring the remaining milk to boil, and pour over the egg mixture. Return to the saucepan, and stir to boil. The preparation can be left at this stage for several days in the refrigerator.
To finish the soufflé:
3. Grease a 7 in/18 cm soufflé dish liberally with soft butter and coat with fine sugar.
4. Warm the custard mixture over a gentle heat, and stir in the pumpkin purée.
5. Whisk the egg whites with sugar, until they form soft peaks. This stage is very important.
6. When the pumpkin custard is boiling, stir in a whiskful of egg white and transfer the custard to a large hand bowl.
7. Give the egg whites a final beating, as they may have lost their smoothness, and

fold them into the custard with a large metal spoon.
Lastly turn the mixture into the prepared soufflé dish, and spread the top level.
If all has gone well, the soufflé should be able to stand for at least 1 hr before baking. This will allow you to make the soufflé well before the main course begins. Have confidence and enjoy yourself.
8. Bake the soufflé in centre oven for 20 mins. Most people enjoy their soufflé a little undercooked in the middle, so don't worry if you think you have messed up the timing. Serve the soufflé immediately at the table.

BUTTER PECAN PIE
Illustrated on page 68

1 × recipe Whole Meal Biscuit Pastry (see page 91)
3 oz/75 g golden granulated sugar
2 tablespoons clear honey
2 tablespoons maple syrup
4 tablespoons double cream
2 oz/50 g butter
6 oz/170 g pecan nuts (or walnuts)

serves 6
Preheat oven 375°F/190°C/gas mark 5

1. Lightly grease a 9 in/23 cm flan ring, and line with biscuit pastry.
Allow to rest 20 mins.
2. Put the sugar, honey and maple syrup into a heavy saucepan.
Melt over a slow heat, then boil rapidly for 5 mins until lightly caramelized.
3. Remove from the heat and carefully add the butter and cream.
Allow to cool slightly and stir in the pecan nuts.
4. Fill the uncooked flan case with the mixture and bake in centre oven for 35–40 mins.
Serve warm or cold with a dribble of fresh cream.
Butter Pecan Pie will keep in an airtight tin for up to 1 week. It does not freeze well.

APPLE AND CINNAMON CUSTARDS

Can I urge you to try these little tartlets filled with fragrant apples, softened with Calvados, cinnamon and clove and held by the most delicate of egg custards. Serve them warm with a little thin cream at your next dinner party.

6 oz/170 g Puff or Short Crust Pastry (see page 90)

1 lb/450 g English dessert apples

1 oz/25 g butter, unsalted

½ teaspoon ground cinnamon

pinch ground clove

4 tablespoons Calvados

CUSTARD:
1 egg (size 3)

1 teaspoon clear honey

3 fl oz/75 ml double cream

serves 4
Preheat oven 400°F/205°C/gas mark 6

1. Lightly grease 8 shallow tartlet moulds.
2. Roll out the pastry as thinly as possible, cut out 8 circles, and line each of the tins. Leave them to rest for 45 mins, and bake them blind for 15–20 mins.
To prepare the apples:
3. Peel, core and finely slice the apples. Throw them into a frying pan with a knob of butter, add spices, and cook apples until soft, shaking them all the time. Lastly add the Calvados. Take care, there may be a few flames.
To prepare the custard:
4. Beat the egg in a small basin with the honey, stir in the cream, and pass through a fine sieve.
For the best results, I would recommend you finish the tartlets off 10 mins before serving.
To finish the custards:
Put a good spoonful of apple into each pre-baked tartlet. Pour in the egg custard, and return to the oven for 10–12 mins, or until the custard has just set.
Serve 2 per person on warmed plates with a little pouring cream as an accompaniment. The above preparations will keep in the refrigerator for 48 hrs or may be frozen for up to 6 weeks.

LITTLE CHOCOLATE POTS

Known in the finest restaurants as Petit Pots de Crème, they have earned themselves a special encore, this time sweetened with a little honey.

1 tablespoon honey

4 tablespoons boiling water

2 oz/50 g dark chocolate

2 egg yolks

1 egg (size 3)

1 pt/600 ml milk

serves 6
Preheat oven 375°F/190°C/gas mark 5

1. Choose 6 little ramekin or petit pot moulds, and set them in a deep sided roasting tray.
2. Dissolve honey in the boiling water, remove from the heat, stir in the chocolate, and add 2 egg yolks, and 1 whole egg.
3. Bring the milk to just below boiling, and pour over the chocolate mixture. Strain through a fine sieve, remove any air bubbles, and pour into the prepared moulds.
4. Fill the roasting tray with boiling water, put a baking sheet over the top of the tray, and bake in centre oven for 20–25 mins. Allow the custards to cool completely before serving. Offer Langues des chats biscuits as an accompaniment (see page 88).
Little Chocolate Pots will keep for several days in the refrigerator. They do not freeze well.

NOVEMBER

Warm Apple Strudel; Chocolate and Walnut Gâteau; Linzer Torten; Crêpes Suzettes with Almonds; Crêpes Normande; Apple Ovals; Hazelnut Eclairs; Dundee Cake; Coffee and Prune Walnuts; Soufflé Rothschild

WARM APPLE STRUDEL

Apple Strudel is just as much fun to make as it is to share with friends on cold November nights.

STRUDEL DOUGH:

10 oz/285 g white bread flour

¼ teaspoon salt

1 egg (size 3)

5 fl oz/150 ml warm water

3 tablespoons olive oil

FILLING:

5 lb/2.3 kg Bramley apples

8 oz/225 g fresh breadcrumbs

1 oz/30 g butter

6 oz/170 g raisins

8 oz/225 g light Muscovado sugar

3 teaspoons ground cinnamon

1 teaspoon ground mixed spice

icing sugar for dusting

serves 8–10
Preheat oven 425°F/220°C/gas mark 7

To make the strudel dough:
1. Sift the flour and salt into a large mixing bowl.
2. Beat the egg into the measured amount of warm water and stir in the olive oil.
3. Add all the liquid to the flour, and bring to a smooth even dough. Cover with cling film, and rest for at least 2 hrs at room temperature. Even better, make the dough the day before you need it.

4. Peel, core and slice the apples thinly, put them in a bowl, and cover with a damp cloth.
5. Fry the breadcrumbs in 3 oz/75 g butter and leave to cool.
Melt the remaining butter, and weigh out the remaining ingredients.
To enlarge the strudel dough:
6. Cover an area 48 × 30 in/65 × 46 cm with a linen cloth, and dust evenly with flour. Lay the well rested strudel dough in the centre of the cloth, and roll out into an even rectangle, 24 × 12 in/61 × 30 cm.
With the backs of the hands, stretch the dough towards the edge, avoiding contact with long finger nails.
Making strudel is always more fun with 2 people, so invite a friend round for the afternoon to give a hand.
When the strudel is thin enough to read the newspaper through, trim the edges with a pair of scissors.
To fill and roll the strudel;
7. Spread the melted butter over ⅔ of the dough, sprinkle on the fried breadcrumbs, again only over ⅔ of the surface.
Scatter the apples over the crumbs, the raisins over the apples, and lastly the sugar and spice.
8. To roll the strudel, take hold of the long side of the cloth nearest the filling, and lift, encouraging the strudel to roll tightly.
Fold the strudel into a long snake, and arrange it onto a paper-lined baking sheet. Brush with melted butter, and bake in centre oven for 35–40 mins.
Dust lightly with icing sugar, and serve immediately with pouring cream or custard. Apple Strudel may be frozen before baking for up to 6 weeks.

Crepe Normande
Recipe on page 75
Coffee and Prune Walnuts
Recipe on page 78

CHOCOLATE AND WALNUT GÂTEAU

WALNUT SPONGE:
3 tablespoons whole meal flour

3 oz/85g ground walnuts

3 oz/85 g ground almonds

4 eggs (size 3)

3 tablespoons clear honey

CHOCOLATE CHEESE FILLING:
5 fl oz/150 ml double cream

7 oz/200 g low fat soft cheese or quark

1 tablespoon clear honey

3 oz/85 g plain chocolate (melted)

TO DECORATE:
walnut halves

1 oz/25 g plain chocolate (grated)

serves 8–10
Preheat oven 400°F/205°C/gas mark 6

1. Lightly grease two 9 in/23 cm sandwich tins, cut out a piece of greaseproof paper to fit into each bottom, and dust with flour.
2. Put the eggs into a large mixing bowl. Warm the honey over a gentle heat, and gradually pour onto the eggs while whisking.
Continue whisking until a thick ribbon can be drawn across the surface, 5–10 mins.
3. Sieve the flour and add with walnuts and almonds to egg and honey and fold in carefully with a large metal spoon.
4. Turn the mixture into the prepared sandwich tins, and bake in centre oven for 25–30 mins. The walnut sponges are cooked when the surface feels springy to the touch. At this stage the sponges may be frozen for 6–8 weeks.
To prepare the cheese filling;
5. Loosely whip the cream and stir into the soft cheese, add the clear honey, and stir in the melted chocolate. Do not over beat the filling.
To assemble the gâteau:
6. Trim the sides of the walnut sponges to make them straight. Rub the resulting crumbs through a coarse sieve and save them for decoration.
Sandwich the two layers of sponge with a thin layer of cheese filling. Cover the top, and sides with the same, saving a little for decoration.
Mask the sides with sponge crumbs, and cover the top with grated chocolate.
7. Pipe 8–10 small rosettes of the reserved filling around the edge, and place half a walnut onto each.
Chocolate and Walnut Gâteau will keep in the refrigerator for up to 3 days.

LINZER TORTEN

Linzer Torten is to the Swiss what Bakewell Tart is to an Englishman. Hazelnuts and cinnamon are baked together inside a delicious pastry flan.

$\frac{1}{2}$ × recipe Hazelnut and Cinnamon Pastry (see page 92)

3 oz/85 g raspberry preserve

FILLING:
4 oz/115 g soft butter

2 oz/50 g soft brown sugar

2 tablespoons clear honey

2 eggs (size 3)

4 oz/115 g ground hazelnuts

TO FINISH:
2 tablespoons clear honey

10 whole hazelnuts (roasted)

serves 6
Preheat oven 400°F/205°C/gas mark 6

1. Lightly grease an 8 in/20 cm flan ring, and line with the pastry. Save the scraps for decoration.
Spread a spoonful of raspberry preserve on the bottom of the flan, and leave to one side.
To prepare the filling;
2. Cream the soft butter, sugar and honey together until pale and fluffy. Use a food mixer or processor for creaming (1 min). Gradually add the eggs, followed by the ground hazelnuts.
3. Spread the filling in the prepared flan, and decorate with strips of leftover pastry.
Bake the flan in centre oven for 45 mins.
To finish the flan;
4. Bring the honey to boil, and glaze the flan surface thinly with a flat brush. Fill each of the spaces with a little raspberry preserve and top each with a whole hazelnut.
Serve Linzer Torten warm or cold with vanilla ice cream at lunch or teatime.
Linzer Torten will keep in an airtight tin for up to 5 days, or will freeze for up to 8 weeks.

CRÊPES SUZETTES WITH ALMONDS

Perhaps the most well known dessert of the French Cuisine. Crêpes Suzettes are served here with a moist filling of almonds and orange blossom honey, quenched with brandy and orange liqueur.

1 × recipe Pancakes (see page 16)

FILLING:
3 oz/85 g soft unsalted butter

2 tablespoons orange blossom honey

1 egg (size 3)

3 oz/85 g ground almonds

1 orange (zest)

1 teaspoon orange flower water

TO FINISH:
3 tablespoons fresh orange juice

2 oz/50 g flaked almonds (toasted)

1 fl oz/30 ml brandy

1 fl oz/30 ml orange liqueur

serves 6
Preheat oven 350°F/180°C/gas mark 4

To prepare the filling:
1. Put the soft butter into a mixing bowl with the honey, and beat until pale in colour. Gradually add the egg, followed by the ground almonds, orange zest, and flower water.
2. Spread a little of this mixture onto each crêpe, roll them up and arrange neatly in a buttered serving dish.
At this stage the crêpes may be kept in the refrigerator for up to 12 hours. They can also be frozen for 6–8 weeks.
To finish the Crêpes Suzettes:
3. Put 3 tablespoons orange juice into the bottom of the serving dish, cover with kitchen foil, and cook for 25–30 mins. Bring them to the table, and pour on the brandy and orange liqueur.

CRÊPES NORMANDE

Every region of France is to its people a manifestation of natural goodness. In Normandy, apples are widely used in local cuisine. Here they are tossed in Normandy butter, moistened with Calvados, rolled in paper thin crêpes, and served with a dribble of fresh cream.

Illustrated on page 72

1 × recipe Pancakes (see page 16)

2 lb/900 g dessert apples

2 oz/50 g Normandy butter

½ teaspoon ground cinnamon

pinch ground cloves

2 fl oz/50 ml Calvados

5 fl oz/150 ml double cream

serves 6
Preheat oven 350°F/180°C/gas mark 4

1. Peel, core and slice the apples. Brown the butter in a large frying pan, add the apples, and toss them lightly for 2–3 mins.
Add the spices, and lastly the Calvados.
Be careful there may be a few flames to contend with.
2. Put a spoonful of the apple mixture onto each crêpe, and roll them up into cigar shapes.
3. Lightly grease an ovenproof serving dish with butter, lay the crêpes into neat rows, and cover with foil.
The crêpes will keep as they are in the refrigerator for 10–12 hrs before serving. They can also be frozen for 6–8 weeks.
To serve Crêpes Normande:
4. Warm in the oven for 25–30 mins. Serve 2 per person with a little fresh cream.

Dundee Cake
Recipe on page 77
Petit Fours
Recipes on page 84, 85

APPLE OVALS

A delicious confection of apples, custard and puff pastry.

$\frac{1}{2}$ × *recipe Puff Pastry (see page 90)*

---

1 lb/450 g English dessert apples

CUSTARD FILLING:
10 fl oz/300 ml milk

---

1 tablespoon clear honey

---

1 tablespoon custard powder

TO GLAZE:
3 tablespoons clear honey

---

serves 10–12
Preheat oven 400°F/205°C/gas mark 6

1. Roll out the pastry into a rectangle, 12 × 6 in/30 × 40 cm and cut out 10–12 4in/10 cm ovals. Leave the shapes to rest while the custard is prepared.
2. Dilute the custard powder with 2 tablespoons cold milk.
Bring the remaining milk to boil with the honey, and thicken in the usual way. Allow the custard to cool completely.
3. Peel, core, and slice the apples thinly. Put a spoonful of custard onto each oval of pastry and arrange the apples to with $\frac{3}{8}$ in/1 cm of the edge.
4. Arrange the ovals on a baking sheet, and bake near the top of the oven for 15–20 mins.
To Glaze;
5. Bring the honey to boil, and glaze pastry thinly with a flat brush. Apple Ovals are best eaten soon after baking, although they will keep for 48 hrs.
Try slices of fresh pear instead of apple for an equally delicious result.

HAZELNUT ECLAIRS
Who could be denied the pleasure of a choux pastry éclair?

1 × recipe Choux Pastry (see page 92)
1 egg (size 3)
CHOCOLATE PASTRY CREAM: 2 egg yolks
10 fl oz/300 ml milk
1 tablespoon soft brown sugar
3 tablespoons plain flour
2 tablespoons cocoa powder
5 fl oz/150 ml double cream
TO DECORATE: 3oz/85 g apricot preserve
4 oz/100 g hazelnuts (chopped and roasted)

makes 12
Preheat oven 425°F/220°C/gas mark 7

1. Lightly grease a large baking sheet with a butter paper.
2. Put the choux pastry into a piping bag fitted with a ½ in/12 mm nozzle and pipe out 12 × 5 in/12 cm éclairs a good finger's width apart.
Brush the éclairs with beaten egg, to which a good pinch of salt has been added.
3. Sprinkle the tray with cold water, and bake near the top of the oven for 40–45 mins. It is essential that the éclairs dry out thoroughly in the oven before cooling.
To prepare the chocolate pastry cream;
3. Separate the egg yolks into a basin, add 2 tablespoons cold milk and the sugar. Whisk in the plain flour and cocoa powder.
4. Bring the milk to boil, and stir into the cocoa mixture. Return the pastry cream to boil, stirring all the time.
Transfer into a clean bowl, and leave to cool.
5. To complete the filling, loosely whip the cream, and blend into the chocolate pastry cream.
To finish the éclairs:
6. Make a split down one side of each éclair, and pipe in the prepared filling.
7. Dilute the apricot preserve with 1 tablespoon water, bring to boil, and dip each éclair first into the preserve and then into the chopped and roasted hazelnuts.
Hazelnut Eclairs are best eaten within 8 hrs of making.
Serve them as a lunch or teatime fancy.
Unfilled éclairs will freeze for up to 8 weeks.

DUNDEE CAKE
The middle of November is the time to prepare the Christmas Dundee Cake, leaving time for it to moisten and mature.
Illustrated on page 76

8 oz/225 g soft butter
8 oz/225 g dark Muscovado sugar
4 eggs (size 3)
4 oz/115 g whole meal flour
2 oz/50 g self raising flour
2 oz/50 g ground almonds
1 egg white
12 oz/350 g sultanas
12 oz/350 g currants
3 oz/85 g orange peel (chopped)
2 oz/50 g glacé cherries (optional)
2 teaspoons orange flower water
4 oz/115 g split almonds

serves 12–15
Preheat oven 400°F/205°C/gas mark 6 then
350°F/180°C/gas mark 4

1. Line an 8 in/20 cm cake tin with a double layer of greaseproof paper 1 in/2.5 cm higher than the tin. Cut a circle of brown paper to fit into the bottom of the tin, and tie a piece around the outside with string.
2. Cream the soft butter and sugar together until pale in colour (1 min in food processor). Add the eggs a little at a time. Sieve the two flours together with the ground almonds, and stir into the egg and butter mixture.
3. Add the remaining dry fruits, and lastly the orange flower water.
4. Turn the cake mixing into the prepared cake tin. Moisten the almonds with a little egg white, and arrange them neatly on the cake. The egg white will encourage an attractive shine on the finished cake.
5. Bake the cake in centre oven for 1 hr, then turn the oven down to for a further 1½–2 hrs. Test the cake with a skewer, if it comes away cleanly the cake is cooked.
6. Turn the cake out onto a cooling wire, leaving the paper on.
When the cake has cooled completely store it in an airtight box for at least 6 weeks before eating. Freezing is not recommended, as the cake can only mature properly at room temperature.
Dundee Cake should be fed on occasions before Christmas with dark rum or brandy.

COFFEE AND PRUNE WALNUTS
Illustrated on page 72

12 oz/350 g large prunes
5 fl oz/150 ml red wine
5 fl oz/150 ml water
1 tablespoon honey
1 orange
1 cinnamon stick
8 whole allspice
FILLING: 3 oz/85 g chopped walnuts
1 tablespoon clear honey
2 pt/1.1 litre Coffee Ice Cream

serves 6

1. Prepare a light syrup from the red wine, honey and water.
Add the zest and juice of 1 orange, the cinnamon, and the allspice.
Add the prunes to the syrup, bring to boil, and leave to cool overnight.
To prepare the filling;
2. Finely chop the walnuts in a food processor, and blend in the clear honey.
Bring to a firm paste, and leave to one side.
3. Remove the stones from the prunes, and stuff them with the walnut paste. Return the prunes to the wine juices until needed.
Serve the prune walnuts warm or cold with Coffee Ice Cream.

SOUFFLÉ ROTHSCHILD

soft butter for greasing
3 oz/85 g candied peel (1st. class)
3 fl oz/75 ml Kirsch
CUSTARD BASE: 5 eggs (size 3) separated
10 fl oz/300 ml milk
4 tablespoons plain flour
1 tablespoon golden granulated sugar
TO LIGHTEN: 5 egg whites (size 3)
3 tablespoons golden granulated sugar

serves 4
Preheat oven 425°F/220°C/gas mark 7

To prepare the soufflé dish:
1. Choose a straight-sided soufflé dish 7 in/18 cm in diameter.
Grease liberally with soft butter.
2. Roughly chop the candied peel, and leave to macerate in the Kirsch.
To prepare the custard base:
3. Separate 5 egg yolks into a basin, add 2 tablespoons cold milk, and whisk in the flour and sugar.
Bring the remaining milk to boil, and pour over the egg mixture. Return to the saucepan, and stir back to boil. This preparation can be left for several days in the refrigerator if not required.
To finish the soufflé:
4. Warm the custard over a gentle heat, and stir in the candied fruits and Kirsch.

Variations on this recipe could be:
Soufflé au Grand Marnier –
      3 fl oz/75 ml Grand Marnier and the zest of 2 oranges.
Soufflé au Citron –
      the zest and juice of 3 lemons
Soufflé au Chocolat –
      3 oz/75 g cocoa powder, 3 tablespoons milk
Soufflé aux Framboise –
      8 oz/225 g raspberry purée

5. The custard must be of a dropping consistency from the spoon.
Whisk the egg whites with the sugar until they form soft peaks. This stage is very important.
6. When the custard is boiling, stir in a whisk full of egg white, transfer the custard into a large hand bowl.
Give the egg whites a final beating as they may have lost some of their smoothness.
Fold the remaining egg white into the custard with a large metal spoon, retaining as much air as possible.
7. Finally turn the mixture into the prepared soufflé dish, and spread the top level with a knife.
Bake the soufflé in centre oven for 20 mins. Most people enjoy their soufflé a little undercooked in the middle, so don't worry if you have missed the timing.
If the soufflé has been made correctly, it will be able to stand for at least 1 hour before serving. This will allow you to make the soufflé well before the main course.
Have confidence, and enjoy yourself.

DECEMBER

Baked Pineapple Bomb; Jalousie Noël;
Oriental Fruit Salad; Lebkuchen Spice Biscuits;
Lemon and Lime Mousseline; Apple and Pear Charlotte;
Apple and Cinnamon Fritters; Chestnut Winter Log;
Storks' Nests; Lemon Yogurt Ice; Assortment of Petits Fours.

BAKED PINEAPPLE BOMB

1 small pineapple
6 Maraschino cherries
2 tablespoons golden syrup
SPONGE FILLING: 4 oz/115 g soft butter
4 oz/115 g soft brown sugar
2 eggs (size 3)
3 oz/85 g whole meal flour
3 oz/85 g plain flour
2 oz/50 g ground almonds
2 oz/50 g chopped candied pineapple
1oz/25 g chopped candied orange peel
2 tablespoons Kirsch or Maraschino

serves 6
Preheat oven 350°F/180°C/gas mark 4

1. Lightly grease a 2 pt/1 litre pudding basin with a little soft butter and put golden syrup into the bottom.
2. To prepare the pineapple, cut off each end with a sharp knife, cut away the outer skin, and remove the central core with an apple corer.
Thinly slice the pineapple, arrange one ring in the bottom of the basin, and the remainder around the side.
Put a Maraschino cherry into the centre of each pineapple, and put bowl to one side.
To prepare the sponge filling;
3. Cream the soft butter and sugar together until pale in colour. Gradually beat in the eggs, if the mixture should separate, add a little flour, and continue mixing.
4. Stir in the remainder of the flour, the almonds, and candied fruit.

Lastly add Kirsch or Maraschino, and turn into the prepared basin. At this stage the pudding will keep in the refrigerator for up to a week, or may be frozen for up to 3 months.
5. To bake the Pineapple Bomb, stand the pudding basin in a roasting tray filled with boiling water, and bake for $1\frac{1}{2}$ hrs.
To serve the pudding, invert a serving dish over the top of the basin, and turn the pudding upside-down.
Bring the Pineapple Bomb to the table with a bowl of whipped cream or yogurt.

LEMON YOGURT ICE

6 fl oz/175 ml fresh lemon juice (4 lemons)
15 fl oz/450 ml natural yogurt
3 oz/85 g icing sugar

serves 6
Adjust freezer to coldest setting.

1. Add lemon juice to the yogurt, and blend in the icing sugar.
Freeze in a metal basin, preferably stainless steel, for 60 mins. Whisk the yogurt ice then and every 20 mins until quite firm. A further $1\frac{1}{2}$ hrs.
If the yogurt ice becomes too firm, leave it in the refrigerator for 20 mins before serving.
Serving suggestions:
Lemon Yogurt Ice becomes very appealing when served with a variety of other sorbets and decorated with an assortment of seasonal fruits. Try Lemon Yogurt Ice topped with a little Crème de Cassis.

Jalousie Noel
Oriental Fruit Salad
Recipes on page 81

JALOUSIE NOËL

1 × recipe Puff Pastry (see page 90)

4 oz/100 g Mince Meat

ALMOND FILLING:
2 oz/50 g soft butter

2 oz/50 g soft brown sugar

1 egg (size 3)

2 oz/50 g ground almonds

2 drops almond essence

TO GLAZE AND FINISH:
1 tablespoon icing sugar

egg, beaten

serves 6
Preheat oven 400°F/205°C/gas mark 6

1. Roll out the puff pastry into a rectangle
10 × 8 in/25 × 20 cm.
Cut the rectangle in half lengthways.
Fold one of the strips in half down the
middle, making sure there is plenty of flour
between the fold.
Make a series of even cuts ⅔ into the pastry
from the folded edge.
Open the pastry out and leave to rest while
the filling is made.
To make the almond filling:
2. Cream the soft butter with the sugar until
pale and fluffy.
Use a food mixer or processor for creaming.
(2–3 mins).
Gradually incorporate the egg, stir in the
ground almonds, and add the almond
essence.
To assemble:
3. Lay the uncut piece of pastry on a paper-
lined baking sheet.
Pipe or spread the almond filling to within 1
in/25 cm of the edge and spoon the
mincemeat over the top.
Moisten the edges with beaten egg, and
position the vented piece of pastry over the
top, sealing the edges firmly.
4. Brush the entire pastry with beaten egg,
and bake centre oven for 40–50 mins.
5. To finish the Jalousie, dust with icing
sugar, and return to the top shelf of the same
oven until lightly caramelized, 2–3 mins.
Serve Jalousie Noël, warm with vanilla ice
cream, or cold as a teatime fancy.
Jalousie Noël will keep in a biscuit tin for
several days, or it may be frozen prior to
baking for up to 6 weeks.

ORIENTAL FRUIT SALAD

Around Christmas time there are a great
variety of new and exotic fruits to be had.
Market stalls are brimming with all sorts of
strange and wonderful fruits; Permison,
Loquats, Prickly pears, Annonas, Guavas,
Lychees, Paw Paws, Mangoes, Bananas, and
Kiwi fruit.
Discover your own exotic combination,
bound in a little orange juice and honey.
Serve with natural yogurt or pouring cream.

LEBKUCHEN SPICE BISCUITS

*In Germany, Lebkuchen biscuits are to be seen in various
shapes and sizes hanging from the Christmas trees. Making
the biscuits is a favourite job with the children. They will be
able to make up lots of different shapes to last the Christmas
season.*

8 oz/225 g whole meal flour

6 oz/170 g self raising flour

pinch salt

5 oz/140 g soft brown sugar

½ teaspoon ground mixed spice

1 teaspoon ground cinnamon

pinch ground cloves

1 teaspoon ground aniseed

1 orange (zest)

3 tablespoons clear honey

4 fl oz/100 ml warm water

TO GLAZE:
1 egg, beaten with a pinch of salt

Preheat oven 400°F/205°C/gas mark 6

1. Sieve the flour and salt into a mixing
bowl, and measure in the sugar and spices.
2. Dissolve the honey into the warm water,
and mix into a stiff dough. Cover, and rest in
the refrigerator for 40 mins.
3. Roll the pastry out onto a floured board,
to a thickness of ⅛ in/3 mm. Cut into various
shapes with biscuit cutters, brush with
beaten egg to which a good pinch of salt has
been added.
Decorate the biscuits with pieces of candied
fruit, nuts and seeds.
4. Bake the biscuit in centre oven for 15–20
mins.
Tie the biscuits with pieces of cotton, and
hang them from the Christmas tree.

LEMON AND LIME MOUSSELINE

A tangy mousseline is often the best thing to round off a heavy winter meal. At present both lemons and limes are of a good flavour.

3 lemons
2 limes
2 teaspoons powdered gelatine
10 fl oz/300 ml natural yogurt
5 fl oz/150 ml double cream
2 egg whites (size 3)
2 tablespoons golden granulated sugar
TOPPING: 2 lemons
1 lime
2 tablespoons golden granulated sugar
1 teaspoon cornflour
TO DECORATE: 5 fl oz/150 ml double cream

serves 6

To prepare the decoration:
1. Remove the zest from the lemons and limes with a citrus zester. Soften the zest in a saucepan of boiling water for 2–3 mins to remove the bitterness.
2. Spread half of the zest on a baking sheet, sprinkle with icing sugar, and toast under a steady grill for about 1 min.
To prepare the mousse:
3. Soften the powdered gelatine in 2 tablespoons cold water, and melt over a saucepan of hot water. Add the juices and zest of the lemons and limes and put to one side.
4. Loosely whip the cream, and blend with the yogurt.
5. Whisk the egg whites with the sugar until they form soft peaks.
6. Fold the setting gelatine into the yogurt and cream.
7. Lastly, fold in the soft egg whites, pour into 6 serving glasses, and leave in the refrigerator to set for 1½–2 hrs.
To prepare the topping:
8. Squeeze the juice of 2 lemons, and 1 lime into a stainless steel saucepan. Add the sugar, and bring to boil.
Dilute the cornflour in 1 tablespoon cold water, and thicken syrup to the consistency of single cream. Allow to cool slightly, and pour onto the setting mousses.
Decorate with a small rosette of whipped cream, and sprinkle with the prepared garnish.
Lemon and Lime Mousses will keep in the refrigerator for up to 48 hrs.

APPLE AND PEAR CHARLOTTE

8 slices buttered brown bread
3 oz/85 g soft butter
1 lb/450 g Cox's Orange Pippins
1 lb/450 g cooking pears
1 orange (zest)
1 teaspoon cinnamon
pinch ground cloves
2 tablespoons brown sugar

serves 6
Preheat oven 425°F/220°C/gas mark 7

1. Line a charlotte mould with overlapping pieces of buttered bread with the butter side outermost.
To prepare the apples and pears:
2. Peel, core and roughly chop the fruit. Sauté with a knob of butter until the juices begin to run.
Cover the frying pan with a lid and continue cooking until soft, 8–10 mins.
3. Add the sugar, and spices to taste.
Spoon the mixture into the prepared mould, and cover with a piece of bread.
At this stage the charlotte will keep in the refrigerator for 48 hrs or may be frozen for up to 8 weeks.
4. Bake the charlotte near the top of the oven for 30–40 mins.
To serve:
Invert a warm serving dish over the mould, and turn over quickly. Bring the charlotte to the table with a quantity of fresh cream or yogurt.

APPLE AND CINNAMON FRITTERS

Just the thing to have with warm custard or pouring cream on a cold winter's day.

1½ lb/675 g Bramley apples

BATTER:
4 oz/115 g 85% whole meal flour

pinch salt

1 oz/25 g butter

5 fl oz/150 ml warm milk

1 egg white (size 3)

1 tablespoon clear honey

TO FINISH:
2 oz/50 g cinnamon sugar

serves 6–8
Preheat deep fryer to 375°F/190°C

1. Sieve the flour and salt into a basin.
2. Brown the butter in a saucepan, add the milk, and warm slightly. Stir in the honey, and add the egg white.
3. Make a well in the centre of the flour, add ¾ of the liquid, and stir into a smooth batter. Add the remaining liquid, and leave to stand for 15–20 mins.
4. Peel, core slice the apples into rings.
5. Dip the apple rings into the batter, and deep fry them for 3–4 mins, or until they float to the surface.
To serve, sprinkle with cinnamon sugar, and serve immediately with thin custard or pouring cream.
As an alternative, try pieces of banana or ripe pineapple.

CHESTNUT WINTER LOGS

A delicious alternative to the portentous Yule Log. Chestnut Winter logs are a purée of chestnuts, rolled inside a whole meal blanket sponge, covered to your desire with dark chocolate.

1 × recipe Blanket Swiss Roll Sponge (see page 93)

CHESTNUT FILLING:
7 oz/200 g chestnut purée (unsweetened)

3 tablespoons milk

2 tablespoons Kirsch or rum

2 tablespoons icing sugar

5 fl oz/150 ml Double cream

TO COVER:
4 oz/100 g plain covering chocolate

serves 6

To prepare the chestnut filling:
1. Put the chestnut purée into a food processor or mixer, and stir in the remaining ingredients to form a soft cream.
Do not over beat.
2. Spread an even layer on the prepared sponge, and roll up tightly.
Trim the ends, and fashion into a log shape.
3. Melt the chocolate over a saucepan of hot water, and spread over the log with a small knife.
Decorate as desired with an assortment of Christmas trimmings.
The Chestnut log will keep in the refrigerator for several days before cutting. Or it may be frozen without the chocolate covering for up to 6 weeks.

STORK'S NESTS

Unusual almond biscuits used to decorate the Christmas tree.

4½ oz/25 g plain flour

1½ tablespoons ground almonds

1 tablespoon icing sugar

1 egg (size 3)

½ lemon (zest)

¼ teaspoon almond essence

12–15 biscuits
Preheat deep fat fryer to 375°F/190°C

1. Sieve the flour, almonds and icing sugar together into a mixing bowl.
Make a well in the centre, add eggs, lemon zest, and almond essence. Stir into a firm dough, cover and rest in the refrigerator for 40 mins.
2. Take a piece of dough no bigger than a cob nut, and roll it out as thinly as possible in a dusting of flour. Make a series of cuts in the dough ¼ in/6 mm apart to within the same distance of the edge.
3. To cook the Stork's Nests, open 3–4 small tins at both ends, and stand them in the bottom of a deep fat fryer.
Drop the pieces of dough into the tins. They will take between 3–4 mins to cook.
Allow them to cool on a napkin, and dust with icing sugar.
Stork's Nests will keep for up to 3 weeks in a cool dry place.

ASSORTMENT OF PETITS FOURS FOR DECEMBER

PETITS FOURS FLORENTINES

$\frac{1}{2}$ × recipe Whole Meal Biscuit Pastry (see page 91)

2 fl oz/50 ml double cream

2 oz/50 g butter

4 oz/115 g golden granulated sugar

3 tablespoons clear honey

3 oz/85 g good quality mixed peel

2 oz/50 g flaked almonds

makes 20
Preheat oven 400°F/205°C/gas mark 6

1. Line a 10 in/25 cm swiss roll tin with greaseproof paper.
2. Roll out the biscuit pastry to a thickness of $\frac{1}{4}$ in/6 mm and cover the bottom and sides of the tin.
Rest for 20 mins, and half bake for 15 mins.
To prepare the topping:
3. Measure the cream, butter, sugar, and honey into a heavy saucepan.
Bring to boil and cook for 5 mins.
Add the mixed peel and stir in the almonds.
4. Spread the mixture onto the half-baked pastry base.
Bake in the top of the oven for 10–12 mins.
Allow the Florentine to cool before cutting into small shapes.
Keep the biscuits between pieces of greaseproof paper in a biscuit tin.

HAZELNUT THINS

3 oz/85 g whole meal flour

3 oz/85 g plain flour

1 teaspoon ground cinnamon

2 oz/50 g golden granulated sugar

4 oz/115 g cool butter

1 egg (size 3)

3 oz/85 g whole hazelnuts (blanched)

makes 20 biscuits
Preheat oven 400°F/205°C/gas mark 6

1. Weigh all of the dry ingredients apart from the hazelnuts into a mixing bowl.
2. Cut the cool butter into small pieces and rub into the dry ingredients to form a crumb consistency.
A food processor can be used for rubbing in but be careful not to overwork it.
2. Incorporate the egg and bring into a fine pastry.
Add the wholE hazelnuts and shape the pastry into a rectangle $1\frac{1}{2}$ in/4 cm thick.
Wrap in cling film and leave to firm in the refrigerator for 60 mins, or the freezer for 30 mins.
3. When the pastry is firm enough, slice as thinly as possible into biscuits.
Arrange on a baking sheet and bake in centre oven for 10–12 mins.
Cool the biscuits on a wire rack and store in a suitable jar.
Hazelnut Thins will keep for up to a week, or the biscuit dough can be frozen for up to 3 months.

FRUIT MEAT PETITS FOURS

6 oz/170 g prunes

6 oz/170 g dried apricots

2 oz/50 g white marzipan

2 tablespoons clear honey

3 oz/85 g chopped nuts

makes 15–20

1. Remove the stones from the prunes and finely chop or mince them with the apricots and the marzipan.
Stir in the honey, and bring to a smooth paste. A little brandy may be added if the paste seems too dry.
2. Shape into little balls, and cover with finely chopped nuts.
Serve Fruit Meats in little paper cases, and offer them at the end of a meal with coffee.
Fruit Meats will keep for several weeks in an airtight tin.

WALNUT PETITS FOURS

Some of the finest walnuts are to be found in the late autumn months. In Switzerland they are made into the most delicious after-dinner petits fours.

4 oz/115 g soft unsalted butter

4 oz/115 g soft brown sugar

1 egg (size 3)

4 oz/115 g plain flour

3 oz/85 g ground walnuts

TO DECORATE:
3 oz/85 g walnut halves

2 oz/50 g plain covering chocolate

makes about 20
Preheat oven 375°F/190°C/gas mark 5

1. Cream the soft butter and sugar together until pale in colour. Use a food mixer or processor for creaming.
Gradually add the egg, followed by the flour and ground walnuts.
2. Line a baking sheet with greaseproof paper, and pipe or shape the mixture into pieces no bigger than a thimble.
Arrange a piece of walnut on each, and bake for 20–25 mins.
To finish the biscuits:
3. Melt the chocolate over a saucepan of hot water, and dip the corner of each biscuit into the chocolate. Leave to set on a piece of greaseproof paper.

AMARETTI BISCUITS

Amaretti biscuits retain the gentle taste of almonds, fresh vanilla, Kirsch, orange and lemon.

1 fresh vanilla pod

1 teaspoon caster sugar

3 oz/85 g soft brown sugar

4 oz/115 g ground almonds

1 teaspoon whole meal flour

½ orange (zest)

½ lemon (zest)

1 egg white (size 3)

3 tablespoons Kirsch

2 teaspoons orange flower water

1 teaspoon almond essence

TO DECORATE:
2 oz/50 g icing sugar

makes 30 small biscuits
Preheat oven 450°F/230°C/gas mark 8

1. Split the fresh vanilla pod open and scrape out the tiny black seeds. Disperse the seeds into caster sugar.
2. Put the remaining sugar, the almonds and the flour into a mixing bowl.
Add the finely grated zest of orange and lemon and moisten with the egg white a little at a time.
Beat the mixture smoothly in a food processor or mixer.
Lastly add the Kirsch, orange flower water and almond essence.
3. Put the almond mixture into a piping bag fitted with a ½ in/12 mm nozzle. Line a baking sheet with nonstick paper and pipe out little mounds no bigger than a grape.
Dust the shapes with icing sugar and leave for 30 mins to dry slightly.
After this time pinch each biscuit from the base using the thumb and forefinger.
4. Bake the biscuits in the top of the oven for 6–8 mins.
If you have used ordinary greaseproof paper and are wondering how you are going to get the biscuits off the paper, see Macaroons page 86.
Amaretti Biscuits will keep for several weeks in an airtight jar. They may be frozen for up to 8 weeks.

HAZELNUT MACAROONS

2 oz/50 g ground hazelnuts
2 oz/50 g ground almonds
3 oz/85 g golden granulated sugar
1 teaspoon baking powder
1 teaspoon ground cinnamon
1 egg white (size 3)

makes 20 small biscuits
Preheat oven 425°F/220°C/gas mark 7

1. Mix all dry ingredients together.
Add the egg white slowly, beating the
mixture well. Use the beater or the blade
fitting of your food mixer for this.
The mixture should be quite firm, never
runny.
2. Line a baking sheet with greaseproof or
Bakewell paper.
Shape the mixture into small rounds and
space out well on the baking sheet.
Brush the biscuits with water and sprinkle
with fine sugar.
Bake the biscuits near the top of the oven for
12–15 mins.
To remove the Macaroons from the paper:
3. Moisten a tea towel with water. Lay the
towel over a very hot baking sheet and
immediately place the biscuits, on the paper,
over the steaming towel. The Macaroons will
keep for several weeks in an airtight jar and
freeze well in little plastic bags.

HAZELNUT SHORTBREADS

8 oz/225 g whole meal flour
4 oz/115 g ground hazelnuts
4 oz/115 g soft brown sugar
1 teaspoon ground cinnamon
6 oz/170 g cool butter

makes 16 small biscuits
Preheat oven 375°F/190°C/gas mark 5

1. Weigh the dry ingredients into a large
mixing bowl.
Rub in the cool butter until the mixture
forms a crumb consistency.
If you are using a mixing machine, use the
hook attachment on the slowest speed, or a
food processor for 3–4 secs.
2. Press the short pastry on a floured board.
Roll out to a thickness of $\frac{1}{2}$ in/15 mm and
cut out into small fancy shapes.
Arrange the shapes on a baking sheet and
bake in centre oven for 30–35 mins.
When the biscuits have cooled store them in
an airtight jar. They will keep for upto 10
days.

FIGAROS

3 oz/85 g icing sugar
6 oz/170 g soft butter
$\frac{1}{2}$ orange (zest)
$\frac{1}{2}$ lemon (zest)
1 egg white (size 3)
8 oz/225 g soft white flour
2 oz/50 g raspberry preserve (sieved)

makes 20 biscuits
Preheat oven 400°F/205°C/gas mark 6

1. Blend the icing sugar into the soft butter.
Use your food mixer or processor for this
stage.
Add the finely grated zest of orange and
lemon.
Gradually beat in the egg white, and stir in
the flour.
2. Pipe the biscuits through a $\frac{3}{8}$ in/10 mm
plain nozzle a good finger's width apart onto
a paper-lined baking sheet.
Dip a melon baller into warm water and
make little indentations in the centre of each
biscuit.
Put the raspberry preserve into a paper
cornet and half fill each centre.
3. Bake the biscuits in centre oven for 10–12
mins.
Allow the biscuits to cool before storing them
in an airtight jar. Figaro biscuits will keep for
up to 10 days although they are at their
most delicious straight out of the oven.

TURKISH DELIGHT
A fragrant reminder of an Eastern promise.

2 tablespoons clear honey
3 tablespoons golden granulated sugar
5 fl oz/150 ml water
1 lemon (zest and juice) or 2 teaspoons orange flower water or 2 teaspoons rose water
2 heaped teaspoons cornflour
0.4 oz/11 g powdered gelatine

TO FINISH:
2 oz cornflour

makes 20 pieces

1. Dissolve the honey and sugar in the water. Add the lemon juice and simmer for 2–3 mins.
2. Dilute the cornflour in 4 tablespoons cold water, and use to thicken the syrup.
3. Soften the powdered gelatine in 4 tablespoons cold water, 2–3 mins. Remove the syrup from the heat, and stir in the gelatine.
Pass through a fine sieve into 6 in/15 cm square tin, and leave to set, 30–40 mins. To finish the Turkish Delight, dust a large chopping board with cornflour. Warm the underside of the tin under a hot tap, 10–15 secs, and release onto the board. Dust with more cornflour, and cut into even squares.

GINGER AND ORANGE FINGERS
These little fingers of orange and ginger are dipped into dark chocolate to complement the fragrance of after-dinner coffee.

6 oz/170 g dark covering chocolate
3 oz/85 g whole stem ginger
3 oz/85 g candied orange peel (uncut)

1. Melt the chocolate over a saucepan of hot water.
2. Drain the stem ginger from its syrup and dry well on a paper towel. Cut the ginger and orange peel into thin strips, and dip into the melted chocolate.
Set the chocolates onto greaseproof paper. Ginger and Orange Fingers will keep for several weeks in a cool dry place. They do not freeze well.

LANGUES DES CHATS BISCUITS

Cats' tongues, as they are translated, are served as a tea biscuit or as a welcoming petit four. Langues des Chats are also well suited to many ice creams and sorbet.

To make the perfect Langues des Chats great care is needed when weighing ingredients. I use letter scales for weighing small quantities of fine ingredients.

2oz/50 g soft butter
2 oz/50 g caster sugar
2 egg whites (size 3)
2 oz/50 g plain cake flour
$\frac{1}{2}$ fresh vanilla pod

Preheat oven 375°F/190°C/gas mark 5

1. Soften the butter to the consistency of half whipped cream.
2. Split the fresh vanilla pod open with a small knife. Scrape out the tiny black seeds. Disperse the seeds in a teaspoon of fine sugar.
Add the vanilla sugar and the remaining sugar to the butter and beat until pale yellow in colour. Langues des Chats biscuits are best made by hand.
3. Beat in the egg whites until quite smooth. Lastly stir in the flour.
4. Choose a $\frac{1}{4}$ in/6 mm plain nozzle and pipe the biscuits onto a nonstick baking sheet.
Bake the biscuits near the top of the oven for 12–15 mins. Remove the biscuits from the tray while they are still warm or they may stick.
Langues des Chats biscuits will keep for up to 10 days in an airtight jar.
They do not freeze well.

GINGER LACE CONES

4 oz/115 g demerara sugar
4 oz/115 g golden syrup
2 oz/50 g whole meal flour
$\frac{1}{2}$ teaspoon ground ginger
$\frac{1}{2}$ orange (zest and juice)
3 oz/85 g soft butter

makes 15 small biscuits
Preheat oven 375°F/190°C/gas mark 5

1. Blend all of the ingredients together into a smooth paste. (1 min. in a food processor).
2. Lightly grease 2 baking sheets with oil, or line with non stick kitchen paper.
Allow 1 tablespoon of mixture per biscuit, 4 to a tray.
Flatten out with a spoon, and bake in centre oven for 10–12 mins.
3. Allow the biscuits to cool slightly, lift them off with a palette knife, and roll each around a cream horn tin (see page 00).
If they become too cool to roll, warm them again in the oven.
Ginger Lace Cones will stay fresh in a biscuit tin for several days, or the mixture will keep in the refrigerator for 2–3 weeks.
Serve as an accompaniment to ice creams, sorbet, and yogurt ices.

BISCUITS PAPILLON

As light and delicate as midsummer butterflies, Papillon Biscuits are served with ice creams, sorbets and yogurt ice.

1 × recipe Puff Pastry (see page 90)
2 oz/50 g golden granulated sugar

Preheat oven to 425°F/220°C/gas mark 7

1. Roll out the puff pastry to a rectangle 10 × 8 in/25 × 20 cm. Cut the pastry into 4 even strips along the short edge. Paint a thin line of water down the centre of each strip and sandwich them all together, pressing lightly in the centre.
Cover the pastry and leave to rest for 1 hr in the refrigerator.
2. Cut the pastry into $\frac{1}{2}$ in/6 mm slices, dip the cut edges in fine sugar, twist in the centre and lay on a lightly greased baking sheet two fingers' width apart.
3. Bake near the top of the oven for 10–12 mins. After this time turn the biscuits over and continue cooking for a further 10 mins. Cool the biscuits on a wire rack.
Papillon Biscuits will freeze for up to 6 weeks prior to baking.
Smaller Papillon Biscuits make attractive petits fours.

ALMOND TUILLE BISCUITS

A classic accompaniment for ice creams and sorbets.

1 egg white
3 tablespoons golden granulated sugar
3 tablespoons plain flour
1 oz/25 g melted butter
1 oz/25 g flaked almonds
½ teaspoon almond essence

makes 8–10 biscuits
Preheat oven 375°F/190°C/gas mark 5

1. Lightly grease and flour 2 baking sheets.
2. Whisk the egg whites with the sugar until stiff.
Fold in the flour, melted butter, flaked almonds, and almond essence.
3. Spoon the mixture into 3 in/7.5 cm rounds, and bake in centre oven for 10–12 mins.
Lift the biscuits while still hot, and cool over a rolling pin. Tuille Biscuits are best kept in an airtight box, 5–6 days.
They do not freeze well.

PALMIER BISCUITS

1 × recipe Puff Pastry (see page 90)
2 oz/50 g golden granulated sugar

makes 20 biscuits
Preheat oven 425°F/200°C/gas mark 7

1. Roll the puff pastry into a 10 in/25 cm square.
Moisten the surface with a little water and sprinkle lightly with sugar.
Fold the two sides halfway towards the middle. Fold over once more, then fold in half completely, like a book.
Wrap in cling film and leave to rest in the refrigerator for at least 60 mins.
2. Cut the biscuits from one end; ¼ in/6 mm is a good thickness.
Dip the cut edges into sugar and arrange on a baking sheet a finger's width apart.
3. Bake the biscuits near the top of the oven for 10–12 mins. After this time turn them over and continue cooking for a further 10 mins.
Cool the biscuits on a wire rack.

FEUILLES D'AUTOMNE
(Autumn Leaves)

4 oz/115 g puff pastry trimmings
3 oz/85 g icing sugar

makes 15–20 biscuits
Preheat oven 400°F/205°C/gas mark 6

1. Roll out the pastry trimmings to a 6 in/-15 cm square.
Brush lightly with water and roll up tightly.
Cover, and rest for 40 mins in the refrigerator.
2. Cut the sausage shape into slices 1¼ in/-6 mm thick and roll out as thinly as possible in plenty of icing sugar.
3. Lay the biscuits on a lightly greased baking sheet and bake near the top of the oven for 6–8 mins. After this time turn the biscuits over and continue cooking for a further 3 mins.
Cool the biscuits on a wire rack.
Feuilles d'Automne will stay fresh for up to 48 hrs if kept in an airtight tin.

SAVOY BISCUITS

2 eggs (size 3)
2 oz/50 g golden granulated sugar
3 tablespoons whole meal flour
3 tablespoons plain flour

makes 20
Preheat oven 425°F/220°C/gas mark 7

1. Weigh the sugar onto a small plate and warm in the oven, 6–8 mins.
2. Line 2 baking sheets with greaseproof paper.
3. Break the eggs into a large mixing bowl, add the warm sugar and whisk until a thick ribbon can be drawn across the surface, 10–12 mins.
4. Sieve the two flours together over the eggs and carefully fold in with a large metal spoon.
5. Spoon the mixture into a piping bag fitted with a 1½ in/12 mm plain tube nozzle and pipe into even lengths, 4 in/10 cm.
Sprinkle with caster sugar and bake near the top of the oven for 10–12 mins.
Allow the biscuits to cool on the paper.
Savoy Biscuits are served with ice creams, sorbets and mousses. They will keep for several weeks in an airtight tin but do not freeze well.

PASTRY

SHORT CRUST PASTRY

Pastry is like a baby, it needs time, patience, and plenty of love.

4 oz/115 g whole meal flour
4 oz/115 g plain flour
½ teaspoon salt
4 oz/115g cool, firm, salted butter
2 fl oz/50 ml cold water

makes 12 oz/350 g

1. Sieve the two flours and the salt into a mixing bowl.
Cut the butter into small pieces, and rub in gently with the fingertips, until the mixture resembles large breadcrumbs. 2 mins with a dough hook (see page 00) or 20 secs in a food processor.
2. Add all of the water, and bring to an even dough; 30 secs dough hook, 10 secs in the food processor.
Cover with cling film, and leave to rest in the refrigerator for 1 hr.
Short Crust Pastry is used for sweet or savoury flans, pie crusts and tarts.
Short Crust Pastry will keep in the refrigerator for up to 5 days, or will freeze for 3 months.

SWEET SHORT CRUST PASTRY

makes 12 oz/350 g

Add 2 tablespoons Light Muscavado sugar to the recipe for Short Crust Pastry, and omit the salt.
Use to line sweet flans, tartlets and pastry cases.

PUFF PASTRY

Crispy flakes of golden air, disappear on a clean, fresh pallet. Why do we bother to make puff pastry? Isn't it more convenient to buy it ready made? More convenient may be, but what about the taste? Commercially-made puff pastries are often made with compound fats and margarines. Such fats do not melt in the mouth as butter does. Instead, an irritating residue is left behind on the palate. Not to be admired. Making your own puff pastry does take practice. A few simple steps in the right direction will help you master your technique.

7 oz/200 g strong bread flour
½ teaspoon salt
7½ oz/210 g cool, firm, unsalted butter
4 fl oz/100 ml cold water

makes 1 lb/ 2oz/500 g

1. Sieve the flour and salt into a mixing bowl.
Rub 1 oz/25 g butter into the flour to form a fine crumb consistency. (Hook attachment of a food mixer, 4–5 mins, or 1 min in a food processor.)
2. Add all of the water at once, and work into a smooth, even dough for 1 min. Cover with cling film, and rest in the refrigerator for at least 1 hr.
3. Roll the dough into a rectangle 8 × 16 in/ 20 × 40 cm.
4. Beat the remaining butter with a rolling pin between 2 pieces of greaseproof paper to a rectangle 3 × 6 in/7 × 14 cm.
5. Place the butter at one corner of the dough, bring the 3 edges of the dough over the butter, and enclose completely by folding in half like a book.
6. Roll the pastry into an even rectangle 8 × 16 in/20 × 40 cm, and fold into 3 as if folding a business letter.
Turn the pastry so that the open end is facing you, and repeat once more.
Cover and rest in the refrigerator for 1 hr.
7. Give the pastry 3 consecutive turns, and rest for a further 1 hr. Before use the pastry must receive a final 6th turn.
After shaping the pastry must be allowed sufficient resting time, at least minimum 4 hrs, preferably overnight. Only then can shrinkage be kept to a minimum.
Puff Pastry will keep in the refrigerator for up to 5 days or will freeze for up to 3 months.
As a delicious alternative, try replacing half of the flour with whole meal bread flour.

Helpful tips for making Puff Pastry:
Conditions must be kept as cool as possible,
early morning is best.
Your best friend when making pastry is a
cold fridge.
Learn to work quickly to eliminate time for
butter to soften.
The butter must be of the same malleability
as the dough.
Butter that is too hard will break into lumps.
Butter that is too soft will leak out during
rolling.
It is essential to allow sufficient resting time.
Most recipes do not stress this point.
Lastly, if at first you do not succeed, try, try
again.

QUARK FLAKY PASTRY

$4\frac{1}{2}$ oz/125 g whole meal flour
$4\frac{1}{2}$ oz/125 g plain flour
$\frac{1}{2}$ teaspoon salt
$7\frac{1}{2}$ oz/210 g cool, firm, unsalted butter
2 oz/50 g quark or low fat soft cheese
$4\frac{1}{2}$ fl oz/120 ml cold water

makes 1¼ lb/620 g

1. Sieve the two flours and the salt into a
mixing bowl.
Add 2 oz/50 g butter, and rub in to form a
crumb consistency. (Hook attachment of
food mixer, 4–5 mins, or 1 min in a food
processor.)
2. Dissolve the quark in the cold water; add
all at once, and work into a smooth even
dough, 1 min. Cover with cling film, and rest
in the refrigerator for ¾ hr.
3. Roll the dough into a rectangle
8 × 16 in/20 × 40 cm.
Cover ⅔ of the pastry with thumb-size pieces
of cool butter and fold the pastry into 3 as if
a business letter.
Turn the pastry so that the open end is
facing you and roll out into a rectangle
8 × 16 in/20 × 40 cm. Repeat the process 3
times, and rest for 1 hr before use.
Quark Flaky Pastry will keep in the
refrigerator for up to 5 days, or will freeze for
3 months.
Use Quark Flaky Pastry for extra light pie
crusts, flans, and delicate pastries, not
suitable for vols au vents.

WHOLE MEAL BISCUIT PASTRY

4 oz/115 g whole meal flour
3 oz/85 g plain flour
4 oz/115 g Cool, salted butter
3 oz/85 g Light Muscovado sugar
1 egg yolk (size 3)

makes 12 oz/350 g

1. Sieve the two flours into a mixing bowl,
and add the sugar.
2. Cut the butter into small pieces, and rub
in to form a fine breadcrumb consistency. (2
mins with a dough hook or 30 secs in a food
processor.)
3. Lastly, stir in the egg yolk, and bring to an
even pastry.
Cover with cling film, and rest in the
refrigerator for 20 mins before use.
Biscuit Pastry will keep in the refrigerator for
up to 1 week or will freeze successfully for 8
weeks.
Allow the pastry to soften before use.
Biscuit Pastry is used in the preparation of
sweet flans, tarts, and pie coverings.

HAZELNUT AND CINNAMON PASTRY

| 3 oz/85 g whole meal flour |
| 3 oz/85 g plain flour |
| 1 oz/25 g ground hazelnuts |
| ½ teaspoon ground cinnamon |
| 4 oz/115 g cool butter (salted) |
| 3 oz/85 g Light Muscovado sugar |
| 1 egg yolk (size 3) |

makes 12 oz/350 g

1. Sieve the flour, ground hazelnuts and cinnamon into a mixing bowl, and add the sugar.
2. Cut the butter into small pieces, and rub into the above to form a fine breadcrumb consistency. (2 mins with a dough hook, 30 secs in a food processor.)
3. Lastly stir in the egg yolk, and bring to an even pastry.
Cover, and rest in the refrigerator for 20 mins.
Hazelnut and Cinnamon Pastry will keep in the refrigerator for up to 1 week or will freeze successfully for 8 weeks.
Allow the pastry to soften before use.
Hazelnut and Cinnamon Pastry is used for making fruit flans, open tartlets, and fine biscuits.

CHOUX PASTRY

| 8 fl oz/250 ml water |
| 3 oz/85 g butter (salted) |
| 3 oz/85 g whole meal flour |
| 2 oz/50 g plain flour |
| 3 eggs (size 3) |

makes 1 lb 5 oz/575 ml

1. Measure the water into a heavy saucepan, add the butter, and bring to the boil.
2. Add both of the flours at once, and stir briskly over heat until the mixture leaves the sides of the saucepan, 1–2 mins.
Transfer the mixture into a mixing bowl or food processor, and allow to cool slightly.
3. Break the eggs into a measuring jug. Gradually add the eggs to the mixture beating all the while until soft and quite firm.
Continue beating a further 3–4 mins.
Choux Pastry will keep for up to 6 hours if covered with a damp cloth, although it is best used when still warm. Choux Pastry freezes well after baking, 6–8 weeks.
Use for profiteroles, fancy pastries, and in the preparation of certain gâteaux.

SPONGES

FATLESS WHISK SPONGE

| 3 eggs (size 3) |
| 3 oz/85 g light Muscovado sugar |
| 3 oz/85 g whole meal flour |
| 3 oz/85 g plain flour |

makes 1 × 8 in/20 cm sponge
Preheat oven 400°F/205°C/gas mark 6

1. Warm the sugar on a small plate in the oven for 6–8 mins.
Lightly grease an 8 in/20 cm cake tin, 2 in/5 cm deep, with soft butter or margarine.
Cut a circle of greaseproof paper to fit into the tin, and dust lightly with flour.
2. Break the eggs into a large mixing bowl, add the warm sugar, and whisk until a thick ribbon can be drawn across the surface, 10–12 mins.
3. Sieve the two flours together over the edges, and fold in carefully with a large metal spoon.
Turn the mixture into the prepared cake tin, and bake in centre oven for 30–35 mins.
The sponge is cooked when springy to the touch, and has receded from the sides of the tin.
Turn the sponge upside-down on to a cooling wire, and leave to settle.
Fatless Whisk Sponges will keep in the refrigerator for 5 days or will freeze successfully for up to 3 months.

CHOCOLATE WHISK SPONGE

3 eggs (size 3)
3 oz/85 g Light Muscovado sugar
4 tablespoons whole meal flour
3 tablespoons cocoa powder
2 tablespoons cornflour

Follow the recipe for Fatless Whisk Sponge (see page 92). Sieve together, and fold in the remaining three ingredients.

COFFEE WHISK SPONGE

Dissolve 2 tablespoons of instant coffee powder into 2 tablespoons of boiling water, and add to the whisking eggs.

BLANKET SWISS ROLL

3 eggs (size 3)
2 oz/50 g light Muscovado sugar
3 tablespoons whole meal flour
3 tablespoons plain flour

makes 10 × 15 in/26 × 38 cm sheet
Preheat oven 425°F/220°C/gas mark 7

1. Line a large baking sheet 10 × 15 in /26 × 38 cm with greaseproof paper.
2. Separate the eggs into 2 clean bowls. Whisk the egg yolks with half of the sugar until pale and quite thick, 6–8 mins. Whisk the egg whites with the remaining sugar until soft peaks can be formed, 3–4 mins.
3. Fold the two mixtures together with a large metal spoon.
4. Sieve the two flours together over the eggs and fold in carefully.
5. Spread the mixture evenly onto the prepared tray, and bake near the top of the oven for 10–12 mins.
Leave the sponge to cool, with the paper still on, face down on a clean tea towel.
Swiss Roll sponges will keep for 3–4 days in the refrigerator or will freeze successfully for up to 6 weeks.

HAZELNUT WHISK SPONGE

3 eggs (size 3)
3 oz/85 g light Muscovado sugar
2 oz/50 g ground hazelnuts
3 tablespoons whole meal flour
3 tablespoons cornflour
1 teaspoon ground cinnamon

Follow the recipe for Fatless Whisk Sponge. Sieve together and fold in the remaining four ingredients.

HAZELNUT AND CINNAMON SWISS ROLL

3 eggs (size 3)
2 oz/50 g Light Muscovado sugar
1 oz/25 g ground hazelnuts
2 tablespoons whole meal flour
1 tablespoon cornflour
1 teaspoon ground cinnamon

makes 10 × 15 in/26 × 38 cm sheet
Preheat oven 425°F/220°C/gas mark 7

Follow the recipe for Blanket Swiss Roll. Sieve together, and fold in the remaining four ingredients.
Hazelnut and Cinnamon Swiss Roll is delicious rolled up with a smooth chocolate filling (see Chocolate Walnut Gâteau page 74).

RICH DARK CHOCOLATE SPONGE

3 eggs (size 3)

2 tablespoons clear honey

1 tablespoon dark Muscovado or Barbados sugar

3 tablespoons ground almonds

2 tablespoons whole meal flour

3 tablespoons cocoa powder

1 tablespoon cornflour

makes 1 × 8 in/20 cm sponge
Preheat oven 400°F/205°C/gas mark 6

1. Lightly grease an 8 in/20 cm cake tin 2 in/5 cm deep with soft butter or margarine.
2. Measure the honey and sugar into a small saucepan, and bring to the boil, 1 min.
3. Break the eggs into a large bowl, and begin whisking at slow speed. Pour in the hot sugar, and continue whisking until a thick ribbon can be drawn across the surface, 10–12 mins.
4. Sieve the dry ingredients together over the eggs, and fold in carefully with a large metal spoon.
5. Turn the mixture into the prepared cake tin, and bake in centre oven for 30–35 mins. The sponge is cooked when springy to the touch, and has receded from the tin. Turn the sponge upside-down on to a cooling wire, and leave to settle.
Will keep in the refrigerator for 5 days, or will freeze for up to 8 weeks.

FINE ALMOND SPONGE

2 oz/50 g soft butter

2 oz/50 g light Muscovado sugar

1 egg (size 3) at room temperature

2 oz/50 g ground almonds

2 drops almond essence

Preheat oven 400°F/200°C/gas mark 6

1. Blend the soft butter and sugar together until pale in colour (1–2 mins in a food processor).
2. Add the almond essence, and gradually beat in the eggs.
Lastly stir in the ground almonds.
This preparation will keep for up to 2 weeks in the refrigerator and has many uses in the preparation of fine pastries, flans, and gâteaux.
To bake the sponge:
3. Line a 9 in/23 cm square cake tin with greaseproof paper, spread in the mixture, and bake in centre oven for 25–30 mins. The cooked sponge will keep for up to 1 week in the refrigerator or will freeze for 8 weeks.

INDEX